The Nature of Science

You Can...

Do What Scientists Do

Meet Dr. Dale Brown Emeagwali. She works as a teacher and researcher at Morgan State University in Baltimore, Maryland. Dr. Emeagwali is a microbiologist, which is a biologist who specializes in studying single-celled organisms, or microorganisms. The goal of her investigations is to gain a better understanding of the processes that take place inside cells. Depending on the question she is investigating, Dr. Emeagwali may observe these living things in nature or conduct an experiment in the laboratory.

Scientists ask questions. Then they answer the questions by investigating and experimenting. Dr. Emeagwali has asked many questions about how microorganisms carry out their life processes, as well as how they affect human health.

In one investigation, she demonstrated that a certain chemical exists in a type of bacteria called *Streptomyces parvulus.* Such discoveries add to the basic knowledge of microbiology. Dr. Emeagwali is pleased, though, when her work has practical applications in medicine. In another experiment, she demonstrated that certain molecules could be used to stop the formation of tumors in people with cancer.

Dr. Emeagwali understands that for each investigation she carries out she must repeat the procedure many times and get the same results before she can conclude that her results are true.

Science investigations involve communicating with other scientists.

In addition to laboratory research, Dr. Emeagwali spends time writing papers about her work in order to communicate with other scientists. She wants other scientists to be able to repeat her investigations in order to check that her results are valid. Dr. Emeagwali also spends time reading about the work of other scientists to keep informed about the progress others have made in microbiology.

You Can...

Think Like a Scientist

The ways scientists ask and answer questions about the world around them is called **scientific inquiry.** Scientific inquiry requires certain attitudes, or approaches to thinking about a problem. To think like a scientist you have to be:

- curious and ask a lot of questions.
- creative and think up new ways to do things.
- able to keep an open mind. That means you consider the ideas of others.
- willing to use measurement, estimation, and other mathematics skills.
- open to changing what you think when your investigation results surprise you.
- willing to question what other people tell you.

What kind of rock is this? How did this rock form? Where did the different materials that make up the rock come from?

Use Critical Thinking

When you think critically, you make decisions about what others tell you or what you read. Is what you heard on TV or read in a magazine a fact or an opinion? A *fact* can be checked to make sure it is true. An *opinion* is what someone thinks about the facts.

Did you ever hear a scientific claim that was hard to believe? When you think, "What evidence is there to support that claim?" you are thinking critically. You'll also think critically when you evaluate investigation results. Observations can be interpreted in many ways. You'll judge whether a conclusion is supported by the data collected.

The book states that a sedimentary rock forms when rock fragments and other sediments are pressed and cemented together.

It looks like fragments of different kinds of rock came together to make this rock. This must be a type of sedimentary rock.

Science Inquiry

Applying scientific inquiry helps you understand the world around you. Suppose you have decided to investigate which color is easiest to see clearly in the dimmest light.

Observe In the evening, as daylight fades, you observe the different colored objects around you. As the light becomes dimmer and dimmer, you notice which color remains clear to your eyes.

Ask a Question When you think about what you saw, heard, or read, you may have questions.

Hypothesis Think about facts you already know. Do you have an idea about the answer? Write it down. That is your *hypothesis*.

Experiment Plan a test that will tell if the hypothesis is true or not. List the materials you will need. Write the steps you will follow. Make sure that you keep all conditions the same except the one you are testing. That condition is called the *variable*.

Conclusion Think about your results. What do they tell you? Did your results support your hypothesis or show it to be false?

Describe your experiment to others. Communicate your results and conclusion.

My Color Experiment

Observe As the light dims, dark colors such as dark blue seem to disappear from sight first.

Ask a question I wonder which color can be seen most clearly in the dimmest light?

Hypothesis Yellow is the color that can be seen most clearly in the dimmest light.

Experiment I'm going to observe several differently colored objects as I dim the light. Then I'm going to observe which color I can see most clearly in the dimmest light.

Conclusion The results support my hypothesis. Yellow is the color that can be seen most clearly in the dimmest light.

Inquiry Process

The methods of science may vary from one area of science to another. Here is a process that some scientists follow to answer questions and make new discoveries.

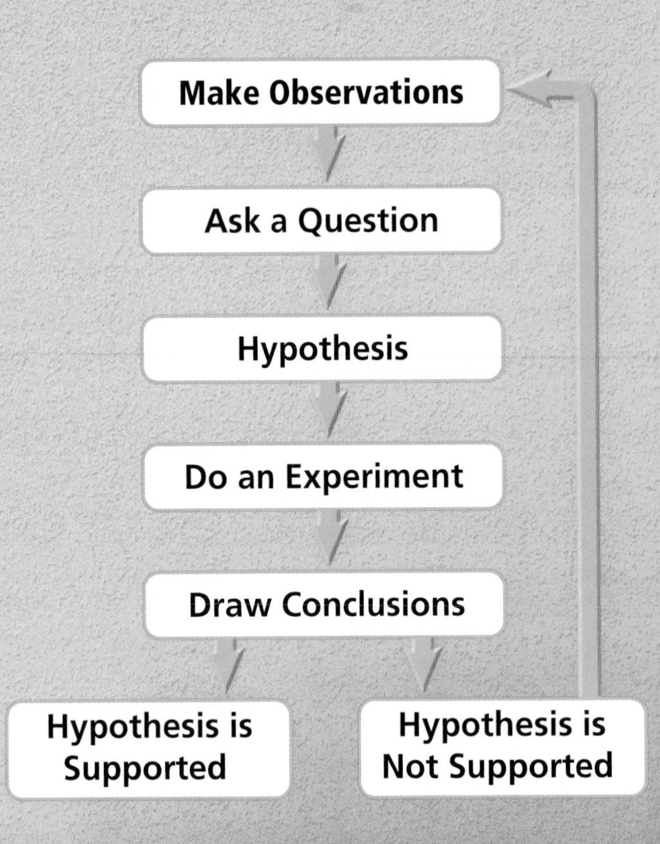

Science Inquiry Skills

You'll use many of these skills of inquiry when you investigate and experiment.

- Ask Questions
- Observe
- Compare
- Classify
- Predict
- Measure
- Hypothesize
- Use Variables
- Experiment
- Use Models
- Communicate
- Use Numbers
- Record Data
- Analyze Data
- Infer
- Collaborate
- Research

Try It Yourself!

Experiment With Energy Beads

When you hold Energy Beads in your fist for a while and then go outdoors and open your hand, the beads change from off-white to many different colors.

1. What questions do you have about the Energy Beads?
2.  How would you find out the answers?
3. How could you use Energy Beads to test a hypothesis?
4. Write your plan for an experiment with one variable using Energy Beads. Predict what will happen.

You Can...

Be an Inventor

Cassandra "Cassie" Wagner became an inventor when she was 11 years old. At that time, she was in middle school. During the summer, she wanted to make a toy for her pet cat. Cats are attracted to catnip, a plant with a strong odor. Cassie considered including catnip as part of her toy.

When Cassie researched about catnip on the Internet, she discovered that some people thought an oil in the plant will repel insects. She could find no proof of that hypothesis, and so she decided to test it herself. In her first experiment, Cassie put a small amount of the oil from catnip onto a cotton ball. She then observed whether mosquitoes were repelled by the ball. They were.

With the help of a University of Florida professor, Cassie ran further experiments in a laboratory. She proved that the spray she made with the catnip oil repelled insects just as well as bug sprays sold in stores.

Cassie called her bug repellent Bugnip, and she planned to have it produced and sold to consumers. In the future, her efforts may lead to other inventions and better ways of repelling bothersome bugs.

"It was over the summer, and I didn't have much going on. I was just fooling around."

What Is Technology?

The tools people make and use, the things they build with tools, and the methods used to accomplish a practical purpose are all **technology**. A toy train set is an example of technology. So is a light rail system that provides transportation in a major city.

Scientists use technology, too. For example, a telescope makes it possible for scientists to see objects far into space that cannot be seen with just the eyes. Scientists also use measurement technology to make their observations more exact.

Many technologies make the world a better place to live. Sometimes, though, a technology that solves one problem can cause other problems. For example, burning coal in power plants provides power for generators that produce electricity for homes, schools, and industries. However, the burning of coal also can cause acid rain, which can be very harmful to living things.

A Better Idea

"I wish I had a better way to ________." How would you fill in the blank? Everyone wishes he or she could do a job more easily or have more fun. Inventors try to make those wishes come true. Inventing or improving an invention requires time and patience.

A company in Canada had a better idea in 1895. It invented the first power tool. Today, many other tools are powered by electricity—including this cordless power screwdriver. Today, inventors are still improving power tool technology, including using lasers and microwaves to drill into steel, stone, and glass. Maybe, someday, you will have a better idea for a new power tool.

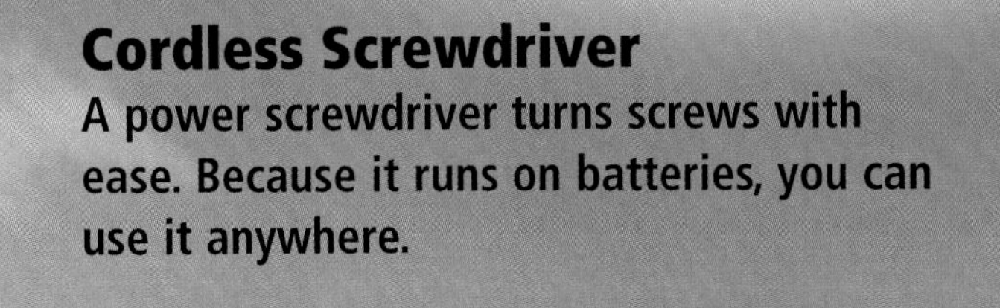

Cordless Screwdriver
A power screwdriver turns screws with ease. Because it runs on batteries, you can use it anywhere.

How to Be an Inventor

1. **Identify a problem.** It may be a problem at school, at home, or in your community.

2. **List ways to solve the problem.** Sometimes the solution is a new tool. Other times it may be a new way of doing an old job or activity.

3. **Choose the best solution.** Decide which idea you predict will work best. Think about which one you can carry out.

4. **Make a sample.** A sample, called a *prototype*, is the first try. Your idea may need many materials or none at all. Choose measuring tools that will help your design work better.

5. **Try out your invention.** Use your prototype, or ask some else to try it. Keep a record of how it works and what problems you find. The more times you try it, the more information you will have.

6. **Improve your invention.** Use what you learned to make your design work better. Draw or write about the changes you made and why you made them.

7. **Share your invention.** Show your invention to others. Explain how it works. Tell how it makes an activity easier or more fun. If it did not work as well as you wanted, tell why.

You Can...

Make Decisions

Trouble for Manatees

Manatees are large, slow-moving marine mammals. An average manatee is about 3 meters long and has a mass of about 500 kilograms. Manatees are gentle plant eaters.

In summer, manatees can be seen along the ocean coasts of Alabama, Georgia, Florida, and South Carolina. In winter, they migrate to the warm waters of bays and rivers along the Gulf Coast of Florida. Living near the coast protects the manatees from diseases they might catch in colder waters. However, there are dangers in living so close to land. The great majority of manatee deaths are caused by collisions with boats. Almost all manatees have scars on their backs from being hit by fast-moving boats.

Deciding What to Do

What can be done to protect manatees from harm?

Here's how to make your decision about the manatees. You can use the same steps to help solve problems in your home, in your school, and in your community.

1. **LEARN** Learn about the problem. Take the time needed to get the facts. You could talk to an expert, read a science book, or explore a website.

2. **LIST** Make a list of actions you could take. Add actions other people could take.

3. **DECIDE** Think about each action on your list. Identify the risks and benefits. Decide which choice is the best one for you, your school or your community.

4. **SHARE** Communicate your decision to others.

Science Safety

- ☑ Know the safety rules of your school and classroom and follow them.
- ☑ Read and follow the safety tips in each Investigate activity.
- ☑ When you plan your own investigations, write down how to keep safe.
- ☑ Know how to clean up and put away science materials. Keep your work area clean, and tell your teacher about spills right away.
- ☑ Know how to safely plug in electrical devices.
- ☑ Wear safety goggles when your teacher tells you.
- ☑ Unless your teacher tells you to, never put any science materials in or near your ears, eyes, or mouth.
- ☑ Wear gloves when handling live animals.
- ☑ Wash your hands when your investigation is done.

Caring for Living Things

- ☑ Learn how to care for the plants and animals in your classroom so that they stay healthy and safe. Learn how to hold animals carefully.

EARTH UNIT C SCIENCE

Earth Systems

Cricket Connection

Visit www.eduplace.com/scp/ to check out *Click*, *Ask*, and *Odyssey* magazine articles and activities.

EARTH UNIT C SCIENCE

Earth Systems

Independent Reading

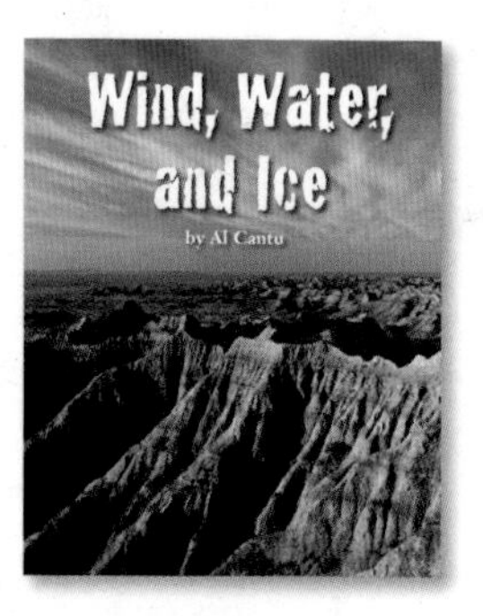

Wind, Water, and Ice

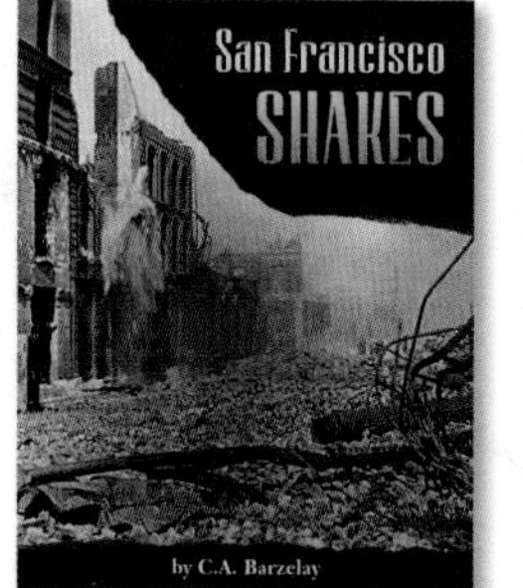

San Francisco Shakes

Global Energy

Discover!

Earth's surface is constantly changing. When a strong earthquake strikes, the surface shakes and rolls. Other earthquakes are hardly felt at all. How do scientists measure the strength of earthquakes? You will have the answer to this question by the end of the unit.

Chapter 6

Earth's Changing Surface

Lesson Preview

LESSON **1**

Features of Earth's surface range from deep ocean trenches to tall mountains. What are these features like?

Read about them in Lesson 1.

LESSON **2**

Wind, water, ice, and gravity—how do these agents wear down Earth's surface?

Read about it in Lesson 2.

LESSON **3**

Shifting sand, bubbling lava, moving crust, and flowing ice—how do they build up Earth's surface?

Read about it in Lesson 3.

Lesson 1

What Makes Up Earth's Surface?

Why It Matters...

The next time you're at the shore, take a close look at the sand along the water's edge. At one time, those tiny grains may have been part of the rocks that made up a hilltop or mountainside. Understanding Earth's different features can help you identify, enjoy, and protect them.

PREPARE TO INVESTIGATE

Inquiry Skill

Compare When you compare, you describe how two or more things are similar and how they are different.

Materials

- modeling clay
- 1 shallow square pan
- paper
- dental floss
- plastic knife

Investigate

Model a Map

Procedure

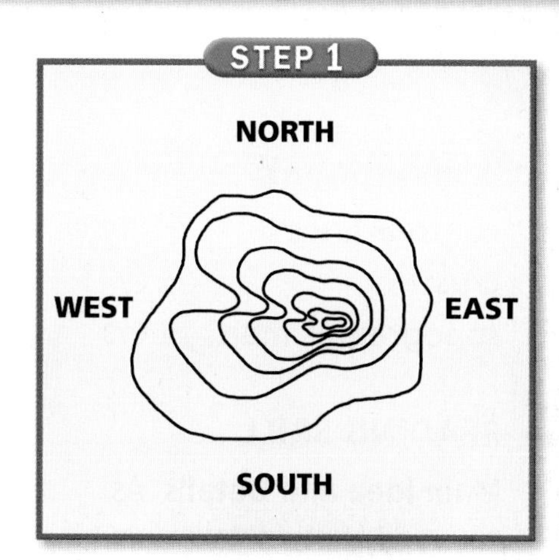

1. **Compare** A topographic map has contour lines. These lines connect points that have the same elevation, which is distance above sea level. Study the topographic map of a hill shown here.

2. **Use Models** Add clay to the pan and make a model of the hill. Refer to the picture and the map.

3. **Measure** With a pencil, mark contour lines on the model hill. Use the topographic map as a guide. Then use a plastic knife or dental floss to slice the hill in layers along the lines. Set each layer aside.

4. **Communicate** Place the largest layer on a sheet of paper and trace around the edges. Then trace the other layers to create a topographic map.

Conclusion

1. **Compare** How are the sliced layers of your model like the contour lines in the map?
2. **Use Models** Look at the topographic map. Where is the steepest slope? Where is the flattest plain?
3. **Infer** How are topographic maps useful? When might you use such a map?

Investigate More!

Design an Experiment
Use clay to model another landform. Cut and trace its layers to make a topographic map.

Learn by Reading

Earth's Features

VOCABULARY

contour lines p. C10
crust p. C7
topographic map p. C10

READING SKILL

Main Idea and Details As you read, write details about Earth's surface features.

MAIN IDEA **Earth's surface includes water and solid landforms. You can identify surface features by their location, shape, and elevation.**

A Watery Planet

Earth is the only planet in our solar system with a large amount of water on its surface. Most of that water is found in the oceans, which are vast bodies of salt water. All of Earth's oceans are connected, forming one great world ocean. Most of the world ocean is in the southern part of the planet.

The world ocean surrounds the continents, which are huge landmasses that rise above the ocean surface. Most of the water on the continents, called inland water, is not salty. Water with little salt is called fresh water. Lakes and rivers are the major surface features that hold or carry fresh water. Rivers, streams, ponds, and other smaller features also hold fresh water.

Plants, humans, and other animals all need fresh water. Yet only about three percent of Earth's water is fresh water. And most of this is found underground or locked in glaciers or ice sheets near Earth's poles. For these reasons, fresh water is a very important resource.

Mountains stand above all other solid surface features.

Earth's Solid Surface

Earth's rocky outer layer is called the **crust.** Different features make up the surface of the crust. These features are found on the continents and on the ocean floor. Continental features are often called landforms.

Mountains are the tallest of Earth's landforms. Their steep slopes rise to tall peaks. Mountains can be found as single peaks or in chains, ranges, and mountain systems. Six major mountain ranges form the Rocky Mountain system.

Hills are smaller than mountains. Although hills do not rise as high as mountains, their rounded crests still stand above the land around them.

Mountain valleys are long, narrow regions of low land between ranges of mountains or hills. Canyons are deep valleys with steep sides. Often a river or stream runs along the bottom of a valley or canyon.

Plateaus are high landforms with fairly flat surfaces. Plateaus are often found along the tops of canyons and can extend for many miles on either side of a canyon. Mesas are similar to plateaus, but are much smaller. The word mesa means "table" in Spanish.

Like plateaus, plains are broad and flat. Unlike plateaus, plains are lower than their surroundings. The Midwest region of the United States contains wide-ranging plains.

As the name suggests, a river valley has a river flowing through it, usually in the center of the valley. The river moves along a channel in the valley floor.

A flood plain is the floor of a river valley on either side of the river. Water covers a flood plain when a river overflows its banks. The flood plains of some river valleys are hundreds of kilometers wide.

MAIN IDEA **Name six of Earth's landforms.**

Plateaus How do plateaus compare to mountains and hills?

River valleys occur in mountains, hills, and plains.

Coastal Features

As you travel from the middle of a continent toward the coast, different landforms appear. In North America, the Atlantic Coastal Plain extends from Canada all the way to Florida. This coastal plain slopes gently from the Appalachian Mountains to the shores of the Atlantic Ocean.

Beaches and marshlands are found at shorelines, where dry land meets the ocean. Beaches are flat landforms along an ocean or large lake. Beach material varies in texture and shape. Some beaches are rocky or pebbly, while others are sandy.

The west coast is very different. There is no coastal plain along the shores of the Pacific Ocean. In many places, the coastline is rocky. Steep cliffs and mountains extend to the water's edge.

Along both coasts, ocean waves pound against the rocky coastline to make many interesting features. These features include beaches, sea caves, sea cliffs, and sea arches.

Pocket beaches form along a rocky coastline. These beaches are small and curve landward, with sand filling spaces, or "pockets," between rocky cliffs. They are common in New England and the Pacific Northwest.

Mainland beaches are quite different from pocket beaches. They are found along straight shorelines that are free of large rocks. Some mainland beaches stretch for miles.

Long, sandy beaches are also found along barrier islands. These islands are separated from the mainland by a narrow, shallow body of water. Barrier beaches may be quite large. Florida's Miami Beach is a large barrier beach. So is the beach at Atlantic City, New Jersey.

Sand dunes are mounds or ridges of sand that the wind often forms along coastlines. They often form in long, irregular rows set back from the water.

Beaches may be rocky, pebbly, or sandy—or a combination of all three.

Coastal plains are low-lying areas that slope gently from the mainland toward the shore.

Ocean Floor Features

Starting at the water's edge, the continental margin extends to the deep ocean floor. This feature consists of three parts: the continental shelf, the continental slope, and the continental rise.

The continental shelf forms the edges of a continent. A shelf normally slopes gradually down from sea level to a depth of less than 200 m (660 ft). The width can range from less than 80 km (48 mi) to more than 1,000 km.

Beyond the shelf is the steeper continental slope. It can fall to depths of 3 km (1.8 mi) and range from 20 km to 100 km wide. The slope forms the sides of the continents. At the bottom of the slope is the continental rise. This region stretches out about 1,000 km across the ocean floor.

The ocean floor has a variety of features, some similar to those found on dry land. For example, Hudson Canyon slices southeast through the continental shelf starting from a point near New York City. Such canyons are known as submarine canyons.

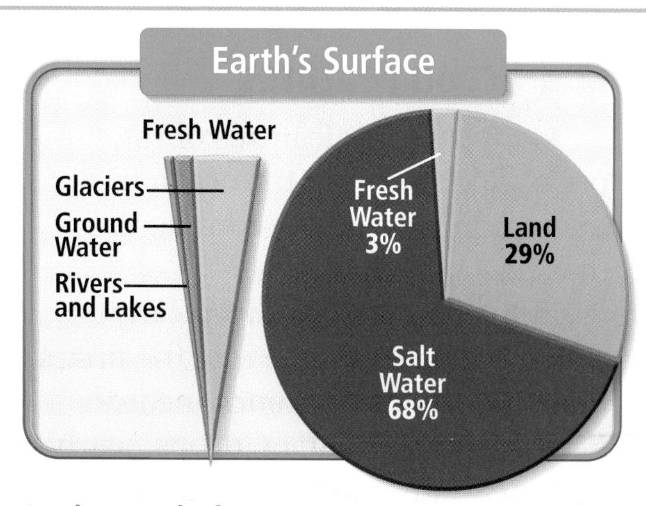

As the graph shows, oceans cover most of Earth's surface.

Mountains and plains are present underwater, too. Seamounts are huge, steep-sided mountains rising from the ocean floor.

Some seamounts have flat tops. They are known as guyots (GEE ohs). They once may have risen above the water's surface. Over time, they were worn down and covered by rising water.

Seamounts occur mainly on the deep ocean floor. This vast area is known as the abyssal plain.

MAIN IDEA **From the shore to the ocean floor, what are the three parts of the continental margin?**

Seamounts may rise thousands of meters above the ocean floor.

Mid-Ocean Features

Many striking features of the ocean floor occur in the ocean basin, the region beyond the continental margin.

In the ocean basin, deep canyons called trenches plunge into the ocean floor. The Mariana Trench, near the Pacific island of Guam, drops nearly 11 km (6.6 mi) below the ocean floor.

Mid-ocean ridges form a mountain chain that runs more than 56,000 km (33,600 mi) through the world ocean. Parts of the chain have different names. These names include the Mid-Atlantic Ridge, the East Pacific Rise, and the Mid-Indian Ridge.

Most mountains in the mid-ocean ridges reach more than 1,500 m (4,950 ft) high. Some peaks stick out of the water as islands.

A number of the ridges have deep, steep-sided valleys down their centers. These valleys create a ragged, rough surface on the ridges. The sides of the ridges slope down to the abyssal plain.

Mapping Surface Features

A **topographic map** is a map that shows the shape of surface features and their elevations, or heights above sea level. **Contour lines** connect points on the map that have the same elevation. By studying contour lines, you can learn the shape and steepness of the land.

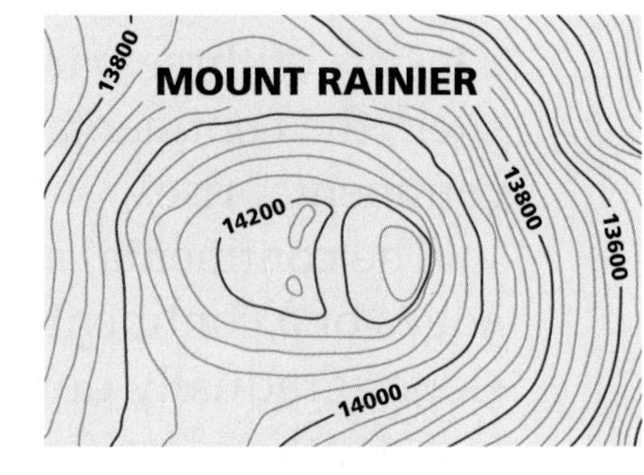

This topographic map shows Mount Rainier in Washington State. The numbers on the contour lines show elevation in feet. The spacing of the lines shows how steeply the land slopes.

MAIN IDEA What do contour lines show about landforms?

Mid-Ocean Ridge The slopes of mid-ocean ridges extend to the abyssal plain.

mid-ocean ridge

Lesson Wrap-Up

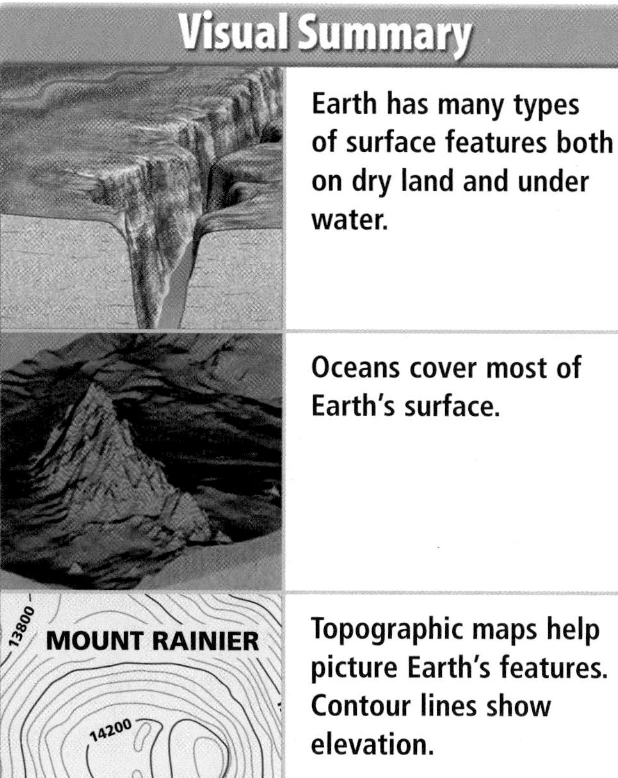

Earth has many types of surface features both on dry land and under water.

Oceans cover most of Earth's surface.

Topographic maps help picture Earth's features. Contour lines show elevation.

LINKS for Home and School

MATH **Calculate and Compare** The mountain chain formed by mid-ocean ridges stretches for more than 56,000 km. How many miles is that? (1 km = 0.6 miles)

TECHNOLOGY **Mapping the Ocean** Scientists map the ocean floor by using sonar, a technology that uses sounds to measure distances. Research sonar and its many uses.

Review

1. **MAIN IDEA** What three properties are used to identify surface features?

2. **VOCABULARY** How do contour lines help you visualize a feature of Earth's solid surface?

3. **READING SKILL: Main Idea and Details** Name and describe the three parts of the continental margin.

4. **CRITICAL THINKING: Analyze** Earth has lots of water. Water covers more than 70 percent of Earth's surface. Even so, water is a critical resource for all living things. Explain why.

5. **INQUIRY SKILL: Compare** Describe how plateaus and plains are similar and how they are different.

TEST PREP

The Mariana Trench is a feature of the floor of the Pacific Ocean. What land feature does its shape most resemble?

A. river valley

B. canyon

C. mountain range

D. beach

Technology

Visit **www.eduplace.com/scp/** to find out more about Earth's features.

How Is Earth's Surface Worn Down?

Why It Matters...

Weathering and erosion change Earth's surface every day. Sometimes these changes take place very quickly, but often they are very slow. The rock formation shown here took thousands of years to form. Understanding how and why Earth changes is the key to preventing or influencing the changes.

PREPARE TO INVESTIGATE

Inquiry Skill

Predict When you predict, you apply facts you know, observations you have made, and cause-and-effect relationships you understand.

Materials

- nail
- mineral kit
- 2 plastic bowls
- eyedropper
- vinegar
- hand lens
- safety goggles

Science and Math Toolbox

For step 4, review **Making a Chart to Organize Data** on page H11.

Investigate

Rock Erosion

Procedure

Safety: Wear goggles during this activity.

1. **Experiment** Using a nail, scratch the calcite over a plastic bowl. In a separate bowl repeat the procedure with halite. There should be a small pile of dust in each bowl.

2. **Predict** What do you think will happen to the minerals when they come in contact with vinegar? Write your predictions in your *Science Notebook.*

3. **Observe** Using an eyedropper, add 3–6 drops of vinegar to the calcite. Using the hand lens, observe the reaction. Do the same in the bowl containing halite. Then wash your hands.

4. **Record Data** Draw a picture of the calcite and halite reactions in your *Science Notebook.*

STEP 1

STEP 3

STEP 4

Conclusion

1. **Compare** How do the reactions of the calcite and the halite differ?

2. **Predict** Based on your data, predict how acid rain can break down or weather rocks. How do your results support this prediction?

3. **Infer** Why are most caves and caverns formed in limestone, a kind of rock made from calcite?

Investigate More!

Design an Experiment
Can water break apart rocks when it freezes into ice? Find out in an experiment with chalk, water, a plastic bag, and a freezer.

Learn by Reading

VOCABULARY

erosion p. C16
sediment p. C14
weathering p. C14

READING SKILL

Sequence Use a diagram to record the sequence of steps in weathering and erosion.

Wearing Down Earth's Surface

MAIN IDEA Destructive forces, such as weathering and erosion, wear down Earth's surface features.

Weathering

Earth's crust is mostly solid rock. The rocks are broken into pieces by processes of **weathering.** Weathering is a destructive force, or a force that breaks down something. There are two types of weathering: mechanical and chemical.

Mechanical weathering is the breaking of larger rocks into smaller pieces of rock, called **sediment.** In cold climates, ice plays a major role in this process. As water freezes, it expands. When water trickles into the cracks of rocks, it can break the rocks apart when it freezes.

Moving air and water also cause mechanical weathering. As blown sand or rushing water hits rocks, the rocks weaken. Over time, they crack or crumble. Even living things can cause mechanical weathering. Plant roots can grow through cracks and break apart rocks. Burrowing animals push against rocks and allow water to move deeper into rocks and soil, where freezing and thawing can weather rocks.

Sometimes rocks will peel into sheets. As soil and rocks are removed from a buried rock, pressure on the rock is reduced. This may allow minerals in the rock to expand. An outer layer of the rock will peel away. Eventually, other layers may also crack and flake.

Trees have the power to move or split rocks as they grow.

Cave Formation

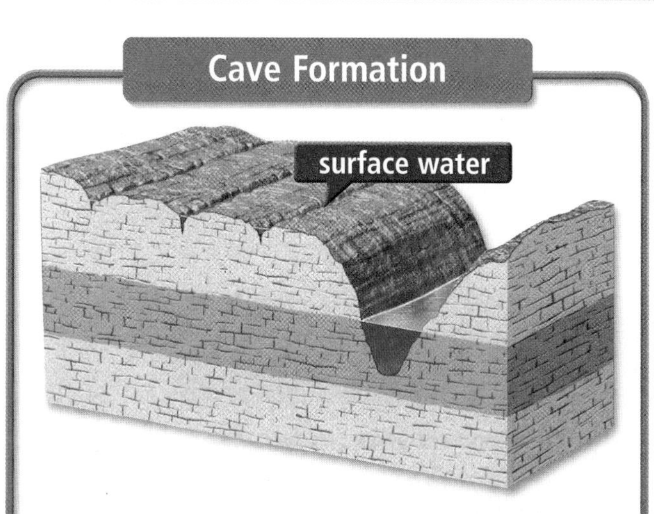

Weak acids formed in rainwater seep into the ground, where they weather rock.

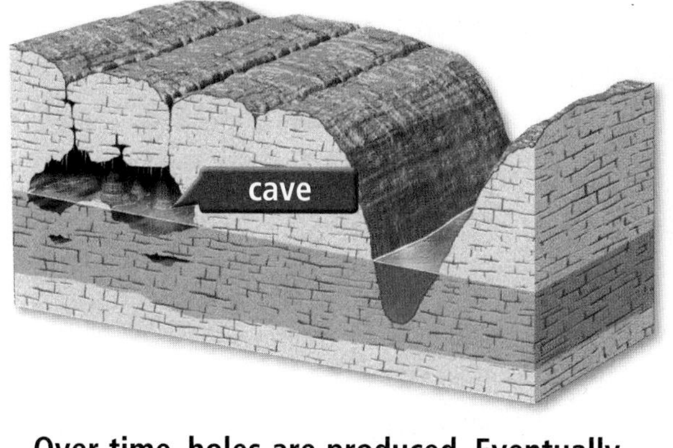

Over time, holes are produced. Eventually, the holes grow into caves.

Caves are a result of weathering. ▲

Although mechanical weathering breaks rocks, it does not change the type of rock. In chemical weathering, rocks change into other materials.

Water is the main factor that causes chemical weathering. Water can dissolve some minerals that make up rocks. Water also dissolves certain chemicals from the air and soil to form a weak acid. This acidic water can easily dissolve certain minerals.

The type of minerals in rock also affects weathering. For example, weak acids dissolve limestone and marble more easily than some other minerals.

Generally, a combination of different types of weathering is at work in a region. Most weathering takes place at or near Earth's surface. However, water trickling through the ground can affect rocks far beneath the surface. Caves are underground hollow areas created by weathering. Large caves are often called caverns.

Most caverns are made from limestone. Weak acids seep into the ground until they reach a zone soaked with water. As the ground water becomes more acidic, it dissolves minerals in the rock.

Over time, holes are produced in the rock. The holes grow, creating passages, chambers, and pits, and eventually become caves. At first, the caves are full of water. Over time, the water drains away.

SEQUENCE **How can water from the surface create a cave?**

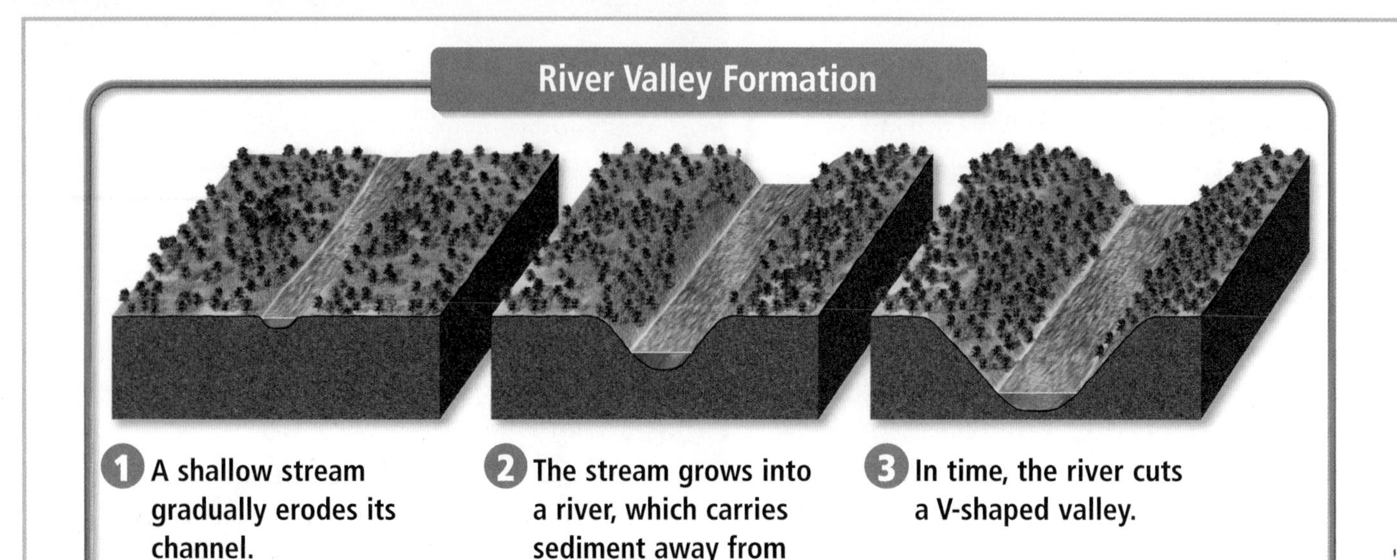

Erosion

Weathering is the process that breaks down rock into smaller pieces called sediments. The carrying away of sediments by moving water, wind, or moving ice is called **erosion.**

A common agent of erosion is water moving down a river. The river begins as a shallow stream, often at a high elevation. Gravity moves the water downhill. As it flows, the rushing water erodes the ground, dissolving minerals and picking up sediments from the streambed. Over time, the river channel becomes wider and deeper.

Usually a stream joins other streams to become a river. The increasing flow of water and tumbling rocks further erode the river channel. This process may carve out a steeper or wider valley. In some cases, rapid cutting of the valley floor in the upper part of a river can create a canyon.

Further along its course, the river gains more water. The water broadens and deepens the river channel.

A mountain stream in California weathers rocks as it rushes over them. It carries sediment downstream. ▲

Over time, rivers create the deep V-shaped valleys known as canyons. ▲

Frozen water also wears down and shapes Earth's surface features. Thousands of years ago, glaciers helped to shape the rolling plains in the northern United States. They also carved out the Great Lakes.

In arctic regions and in high mountains, glaciers continue to shape Earth today. Gravity moves rivers of ice downhill toward the sea. Although glaciers move very slowly, their weight and size give them great power. Mountain glaciers can transform V-shaped river valleys into U-shaped valleys.

Glaciers can also move enormous amounts of soil and rock. These sediments are carried along the bottoms and sides of the ice. As the ice inches forward, sediments in the ice grind against the surface below.

Glaciers often carve out hollows in the land they erode. When the glaciers melt, these hollows fill with water to form lakes. Glaciers created more than 10,000 such lakes in Minnesota.

Ocean waves and currents also erode Earth's surface. Crashing waves break down rock along coastlines. The sediments are dragged back and forth, slowly turning to sand.

Wind and waves from the open ocean also batter headlands. Headlands are narrow sections of land that jut out into the ocean. Usually they are cliffs of hard rock.

Waves curve around the headland, throwing up salty water and pebbles. Gradually this movement erodes cracks in the headlands, forming sea caves. Sea caves on both sides of a headland may join to form a sea arch.

As erosion continues, the top of the arch may collapse. The ocean side of the arch is left standing alone. This single column is called a sea stack.

SEQUENCE **Describe one way that erosion wears down Earth's surface.**

A sea arch forms when sea caves on both sides of a headland join. ▼

Melting glaciers left many lakes behind. ▲

Slow and Fast Changes

The ongoing process of erosion keeps the landscape changing. In general, such destructive forces act very slowly. However, sometimes such changes happen much faster.

You read that chemical weathering creates caves in certain types of rock beneath Earth's surface. This process can take thousands of years. However, after a cave has formed, the rock above the cave often has little support. At some point, this rock may collapse, forming a sinkhole.

Sinkholes can form very suddenly. One large sinkhole formed in a single day in Winter Park, Florida. The city sealed it and made an urban lake.

***Sinkhole* is a very descriptive term: Land above weathered rock sinks into a hole. This sinkhole affected central Florida. ▲**

When sediments slide down a steep slope, buildings on them slide, too. This landslide took place in southern California. ▼

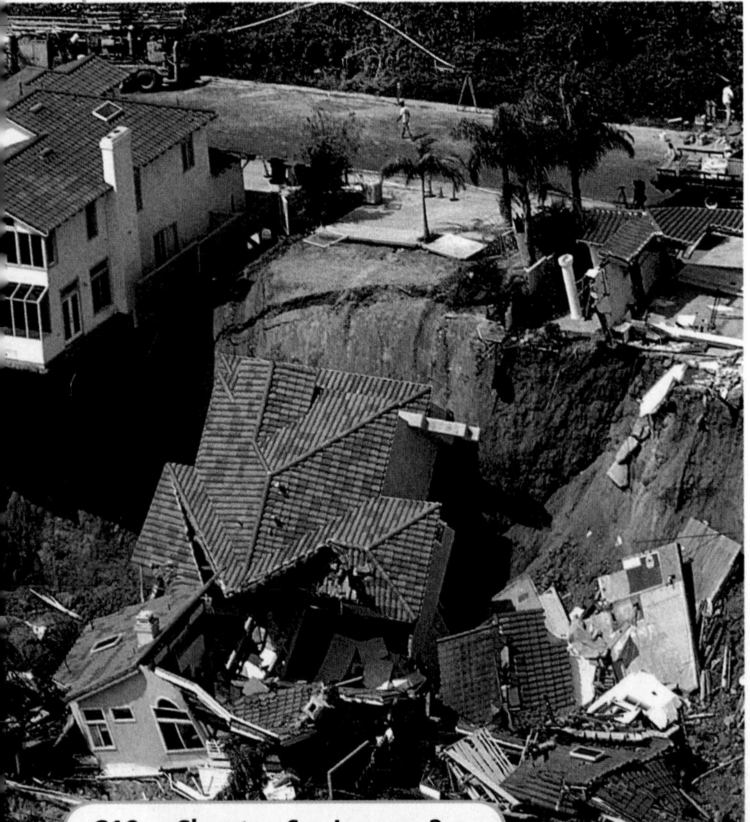

Landslides also occur suddenly as the result of erosion. In fact, they can happen in minutes. Landslides are large movements of land that tumble down a steep slope. Mudslides, rock falls, and avalanches are examples of landslides.

Although gravity is the main cause of a landslide, other destructive forces are involved. Erosion from rivers, rain, glaciers, or ocean water may steepen a slope and loosen sediments. If the sediments become soaked with water, they may slide more easily. Any disturbance, such as a minor earthquake, can create cracks or shake rocks loose. This action can start landslides.

Volcanoes can also cause landslides. Volcanic eruptions can deposit ash and other materials on steep slopes. Heavy rains added to this material can cause a landslide.

SEQUENCE **How does a landslide occur?**

Lesson Wrap-Up

Visual Summary

Earth's surface features are worn down by destructive forces, such as weathering and erosion.

Water, wind, and the actions of plants and animals all can cause weathering.

In erosion, weathered rock is moved by wind, water, ice, or gravity.

Destructive forces usually act to change Earth's surface slowly but can also cause rapid changes to Earth's surface.

MATH **Solve a Problem** You observe a giant wave crash on the rocks. After 1.5 seconds, you hear the sound of the crashing wave. How far are you from the rocks? (Speed of sound in air is 340 m/sec.)

WRITING **Narrative** Plan a trip to the Grand Canyon, Glacier National Park, or Carlsbad Caverns. Research your chosen park. What activities will you participate in? What sights will you see?

Review

1. **MAIN IDEA** Why are weathering and erosion considered destructive forces?
2. **VOCABULARY** What are sediments? Give an example of sediments and how they form.
3. **READING SKILL: Sequence** Describe the sequence of events in the formation of a cave.
4. **CRITICAL THINKING: Infer** How could you tell if a glacier had once moved across a region?
5. **INQUIRY SKILL: Predict** Would the features of a marble statue last longer in a dry desert region or in a warm, moist region that has heavy industry? Explain your reasoning.

TEST PREP

Which of these is the strongest agent of chemical weathering?

A. plant roots

B. acidic water

C. burrowing animals

D. freezing water

Technology

Visit **www.eduplace.com/scp/** to find out more about erosion and weathering.

Focus On

Primary Source

Cleopatra's Needle

How can weathering and erosion change rock? One ancient stone obelisk—a kind of tall statue—provides a very interesting example.

In appreciation for help in building the Suez Canal, the ruler of Egypt presented the United States an obelisk that was more than 3,000 years old. This obelisk is now called Cleopatra's Needle. It was installed in Central Park in New York City in 1881.

The obelisk remains in the same spot today, but it has changed drastically. Much of the outer surface of the stone has worn away, blurring inscriptions that were clear when the statue arrived.

Look at the photos of Cleopatra's Needle and a similar obelisk that remained in Egypt. In 1881, the two looked much alike. How are they different now? How do you explain these differences? For a hint, compare the graphs of temperature and precipitation in the two locations.

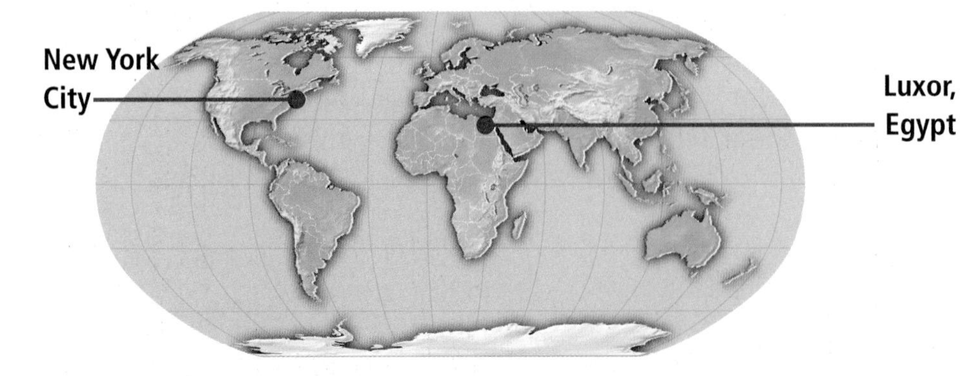

New York City
Cleopatra's Needle was moved in 1881 from Egypt to New York City.

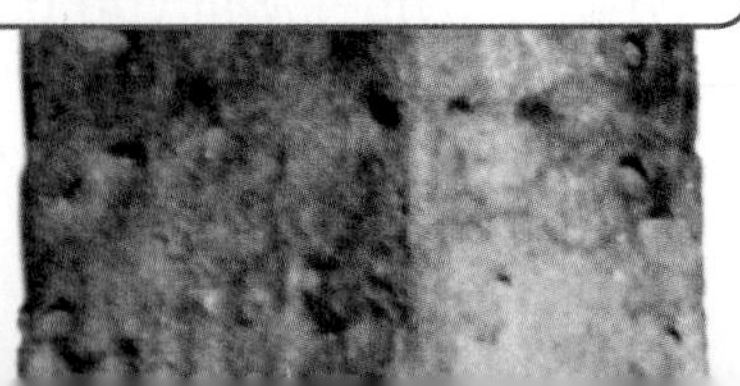

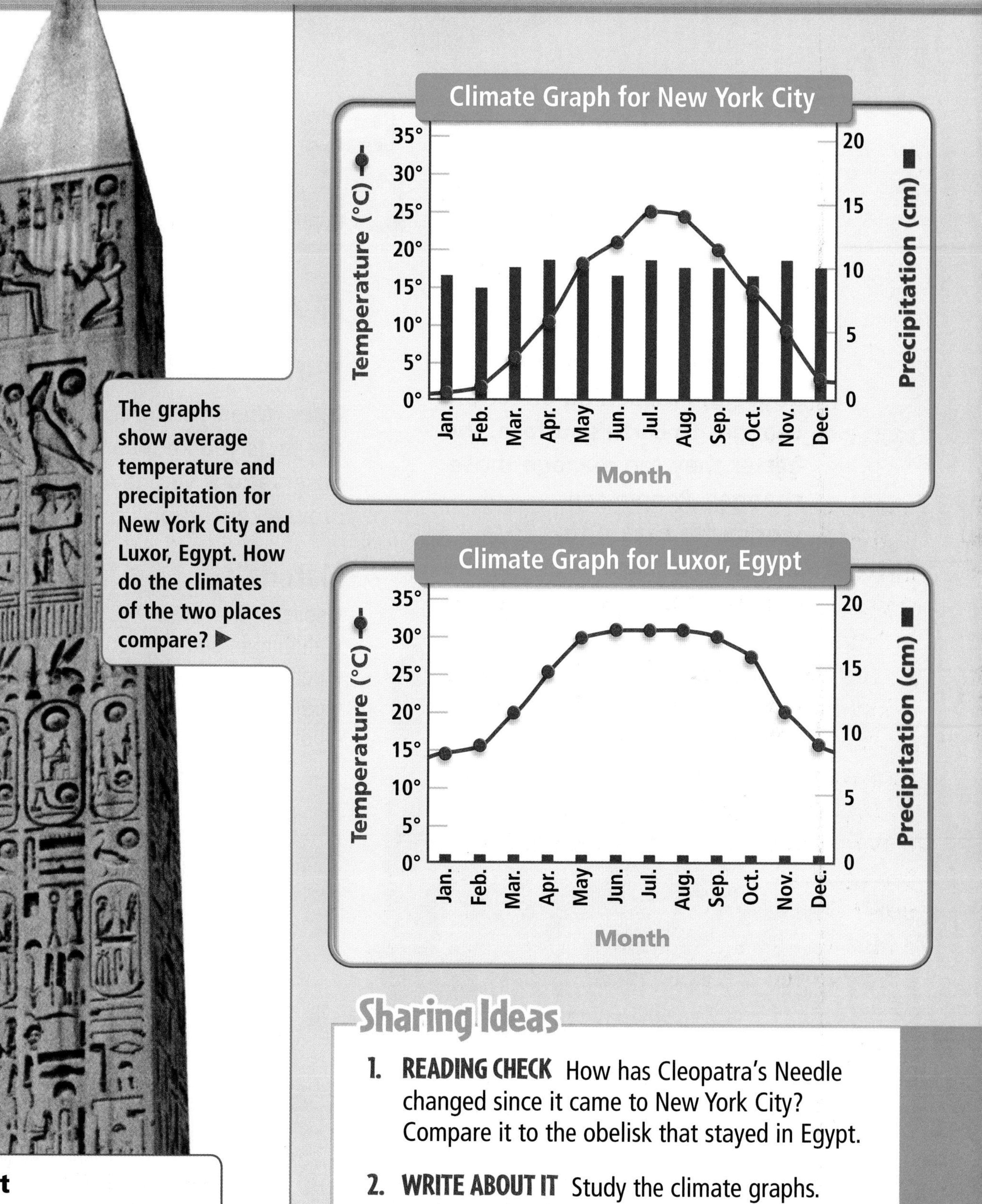

The graphs show average temperature and precipitation for New York City and Luxor, Egypt. How do the climates of the two places compare? ▶

Egypt
The Obelisk of Ramesses II has remained in Egypt since ancient times.

Sharing Ideas

1. **READING CHECK** How has Cleopatra's Needle changed since it came to New York City? Compare it to the obelisk that stayed in Egypt.
2. **WRITE ABOUT IT** Study the climate graphs. Compare the climates of the two places.
3. **TALK ABOUT IT** How do you explain the differences between the two statues?

Lesson 3

How Is Earth's Surface Built Up?

Why It Matters...

The more people understand about the cause and effect of changes to Earth's surface, the better they can manage those changes. People can work with nature to take care of Earth's surface and enjoy its features.

PREPARE TO INVESTIGATE

Inquiry Skill

Infer When you infer, you use facts you know and observations you have made to draw a conclusion.

Materials

- soil
- aluminum pan
- pencil
- paper cup
- bottle of water

Investigate

Set Up a Streaming Slope

Procedure

STEP 1

STEP 4

1. **Use Models** With a partner, build a soil slope on one end of an aluminum pan. The slope can be steep or gentle.
2. **Record Data** Draw a picture of the soil slope in your *Science Notebook.*
3. **Predict** You will drip water from a paper cup onto the soil at the top of the slope. Predict what you think will happen. Record your prediction.
4. **Experiment** With a pencil, poke a small hole in the bottom of a paper cup. Cover the hole in the cup with your finger. Have your partner fill the cup with water from a water bottle. Hold the cup 3 to 4 cm above the soil at the top of the slope. Remove your finger and let the water flow over the soil slope.
5. **Observe** What happened to the soil? Draw a picture and describe the changes in your *Science Notebook.*

Conclusion

1. **Compare** Look at the two pictures you drew of the soil slope. How are they alike and different? Do the pictures support your prediction about what would happen when you poured water onto the slope?
2. **Infer** What can you infer about the way water and gravity wear down and build up Earth's surface?

Investigate More!

Design an Experiment
Make another soil slope. This time, pour water from the bottle down the slope. How do the speed and amount of water affect a soil slope?

Learn by Reading

VOCABULARY

deposition p. C24

READING SKILL

Cause and Effect Use a chart to show the effects of constructive forces on Earth's surface.

Building Up Earth's Surface

MAIN IDEA Forces such as deposition and volcanic activity build up Earth's surface features.

Deposition

Have you seen waves gently lapping at a sandy beach? Waves are part of the reason that beaches have sand. Ocean waves and currents drop sand on a beach in a process called deposition.

Deposition is the dropping, or releasing, of sediments that have been moved from one place to another. Sand is sediment made from rocks or shells that have been ground into fine grains.

Both erosion and deposition are gradual processes. However, erosion is a destructive force, meaning that it wears down the land. Deposition is a constructive force, meaning that it builds up the land.

Wind sweeps sand into sand dunes. Sand dunes are sediment deposits that form on the inland part of beaches.

Deposition helps create a variety of surface features. Several of these features occur as part of river systems.

Recall that the source of a river is usually inland at some high elevation. The water flows downhill, swiftly at first, picking up sediment. At the mouth of the river, the water usually empties into a large body of water, such as a lake or ocean.

As it nears the mouth, the land gradually levels out. The leveling causes the water to lose energy and slow down. Sediment drops out of the water.

When a river moves across wide, flat regions, the river begins to wind in smooth curves called meanders. Meanders increase in size as water erodes the outside of each curve and deposits sediment on the inside.

Flooding of rivers on lowlands also deposits sediment. This sediment builds up on the flood plains.

When the flow of river water decreases quickly, special kinds of deposits are formed. An alluvial fan is a fan-shaped land mass that forms after a river rushes down a steep slope, then slows over a flat plain.

A delta is a low plain that forms where a river enters an ocean. If the river is large, the delta will be large, too. The mighty Mississippi River has a vast delta that extends well out into the Gulf of Mexico.

CAUSE AND EFFECT **Why is sediment deposited as the slope of a river bed levels out?**

Alluvial fans and deltas are formed when rivers slow suddenly and their sediments are deposited. ▲

As a river flows across a flat plain, its course begins to wind in curves called meanders. ▲

Pushing Up Earth's Surface

Surface features can be pushed up from below as well as built up from above. Not far below Earth's surface, temperatures are quite high. In some places, the conditions are hot enough to melt rock!

Melted rock below Earth's surface is called magma. Magma originates in a layer of Earth just below the crust. Pressure below the surface can cause magma to push up on Earth's crust, creating round, dome-shaped mountains.

In some places, magma can work its way up through the crust and flow out onto Earth's surface as lava. As lava flows, it cools and hardens into rock.

In some places, enough lava will build up to form a huge deposit with gently sloping sides. Such deposits are called shield cones. Shield cones often form on the ocean floor. For example, the Hawaiian Islands are actually the tops of several giant shield cones. The base of Mauna Loa, the largest of these cones, is about 4,500 m (15,000 ft) below the surface of the Pacific Ocean. Its peak rises over 4,100 m (14,000 ft) above the ocean's surface.

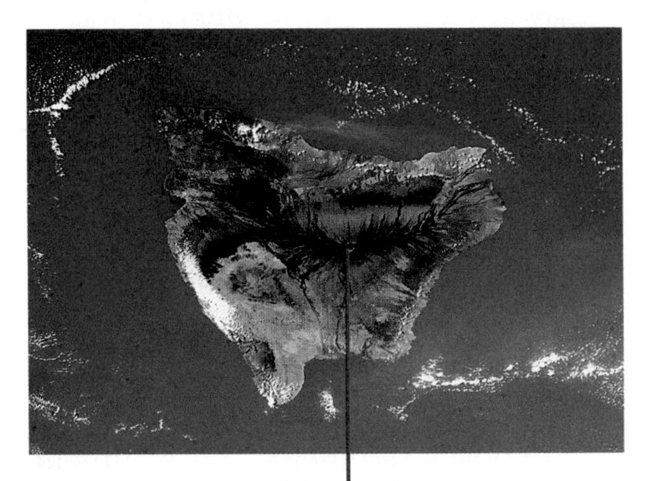

Compare this view of Hawaii from the International Space Station to the illustration below. ▶

Mauna Loa

Crust

Mantle

The crust moves over the mantle.

Hot spot

Building Islands

The Hawaiian Islands consist of a series of shield cones that extend from the floor of the Pacific Ocean to well above its surface. As the crust continues to move over the magma dome, new mountains form. ▲

Building Mountains

1 **The Himalayas began forming when one plate of Earth's crust crashed into another plate.**

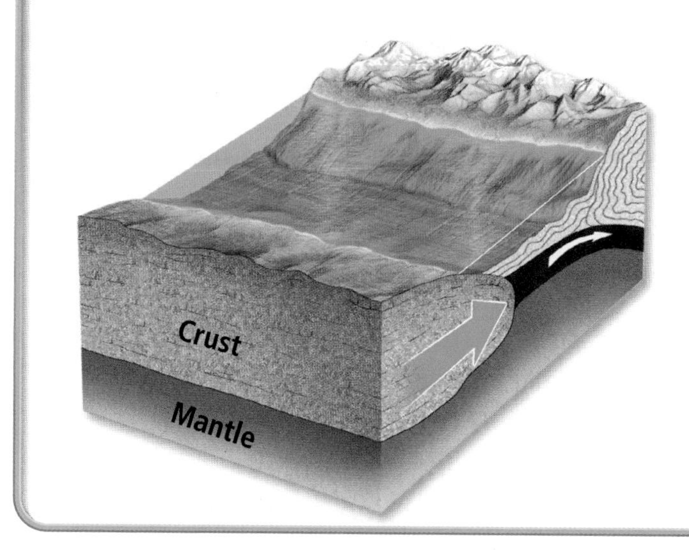

2 **For millions of years, the plates have continued to push together, folding and uplifting to form mountains.**

A different constructive force created the Himalaya Mountains. These mountains in Central Asia are among the highest on Earth.

The Himalayas began forming about 65 million years ago when huge sections of Earth's crust moved into each other. The pressure caused the crust to fold.

Other features of Earth are made from the remains of living things. For example, the chalk cliffs of Dover, England, are made up of shells of tiny sea animals. These shells were deposited on the sea floor millions of years ago. When forces below the crust raised the sea floor, the chalk deposits became chalk cliffs.

Coral reefs are another type of formation produced from the remains of living things. In shallow tropical waters, tiny animals called corals gather in colonies. As corals die, their skeletons build up into a bumpy ridge called a reef.

In some Pacific Ocean waters, reefs are built around volcanic islands. Sometimes an island will sink, but the coral continues to grow. This creates a barrier reef separate from the island.

CAUSE AND EFFECT **How were the Himalaya Mountains formed?**

Atolls are ring-shaped islands formed from deposits of coral skeletons called coral reefs. ▶

Glacial Deposits

Thousands of years ago, snow fell year-round over large areas of Asia, Europe, and North America. Over time, the weight of snow from the top added pressure below. Slowly, the snow turned to ice. Glaciers were formed.

The ice in some of these glaciers was almost a thousand meters thick. The ice's weight became so great that it pushed and dented the land.

These moving masses of ice were tremendous forces of erosion. Huge amounts of soil and rock were pushed ahead of the ice and carried along in the glacier's bottom layers.

After thousands of years, the ice began to melt. The glaciers reached their present positions about 11,000 years ago. As the ice melted, it left behind a changed landscape.

The rock material deposited by a glacier is known as till. Till may be silt, sand, gravel, boulders, or sharp rocks. Some till is picked up as a glacier scrapes Earth's surface. The glacier drags till along its icy base.

Eskers form from streams that flow along the bottoms of melting glaciers. ▲

A glacier also deposits till at its front, or snout. Such deposits are called moraines. Long Island, New York, is the terminal moraine left when the last ice sheet melted. The melting water carried sand and clay away from the snout. Today, the southern portion of Long Island is sandy, while the northern portion is rocky.

Streams flowing through tunnels in melting glaciers deposit sand and gravel in ridges, too. These winding ridges are called eskers.

CAUSE AND EFFECT **How do glaciers deposit sediment?**

Cirque

In high mountains, glaciers can carve out bowl-shaped hollows called cirques. ◄

Lesson Wrap-Up

Visual Summary

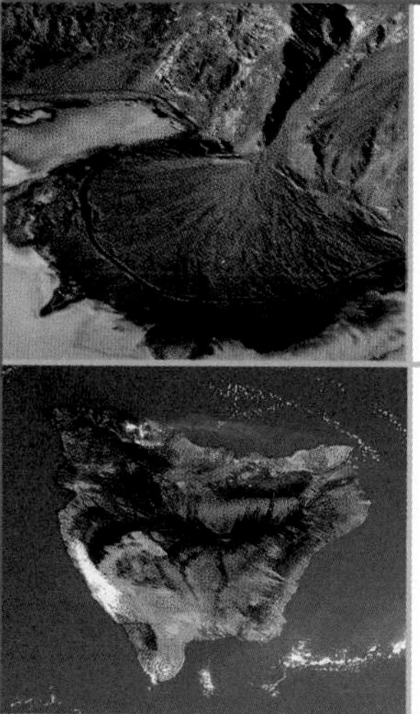

Deposition builds up surface features such as sand dunes, alluvial fans, and river deltas.

Magma pushing up from Earth's mantle can create islands and mountains.

Mountains can also form when tectonic plates collide, folding and lifting upward.

Cirques, moraines, and eskers are formed by glacial deposits.

LINKS for Home and School

MATH **Solve a Problem** A particular glacier moves about eight centimeters a year. At this rate, how long will it take the glacier to move one kilometer?

SOCIAL STUDIES **Make a Map** The state of Hawaii is made up of a chain of islands. Research Hawaii. What unusual plants and animals live there? What are some benefits and challenges of living on an island? Create a poster to present your findings.

Review

1. **MAIN IDEA** Compare Earth's constructive forces and destructive forces.
2. **VOCABULARY** Why is deposition described as the opposite of erosion? Give examples of these processes.
3. **READING SKILL: Cause and Effect** What causes the creation of dome mountains?
4. **CRITICAL THINKING: Synthesizing** In Hawaii, some beaches are covered in black sand. What can you conclude from this fact?
5. **INQUIRY SKILL: Infer** What can the size and shape of a sand dune tell you about how it was formed?

TEST PREP

When a river meets an ocean, sediments drop out of the river because the river

A. speeds up.

B. slows down.

C. becomes saltier.

D. flows uphill.

Technology

Visit **www.eduplace.com/scp/** to find out more about building up Earth's surface.

Extreme Science

Masterpiece of Erosion

What a drop! You're looking down into one of the deepest canyons in the world. In fact, this canyon system is so deep and vast it was named the Grand Canyon.

How did the Grand Canyon form? Erosion. The Colorado River has been steadily wearing its way into the plateau underneath it for millions of years. Wind, rain, gravity and other forces have helped shape the canyon walls. The result is a natural wonder. The Grand Canyon winds more than 270 miles at an average depth of 4,000 feet. In some places, if you could throw a rock far enough out, it would fall more than a mile before hitting bottom.

READING LINK: Compare and Contrast

At the Grand Canyon's deepest point, it would take four and a half Empire State Buildings stacked on top of each other to reach the rim!

Vocabulary

Complete each sentence with a term from the list. You may use each term more than once.

contour lines C10
crust C7
deposition C24
erosion C16
sediment C14
topographic map C10
weathering C14

1. ____ is a constructive force.
2. A map that shows the shapes of Earth's landforms is a ____.
3. The rocky outer layer of Earth is called the ____.
4. A topographic map has ____ that connect places that have the same elevation.
5. Weathering and ____ are destructive forces.
6. Moving water, wind, and ice carry weathered rocks away in a process called ____.
7. Sand and other tiny pieces of rock are moved by erosion and settled by ____.
8. Tiny pieces that form from the weathering of rocks are ____.
9. Water is a common agent of both weathering and ____.
10. The process known as ____ can be mechanical or chemical.

Test Prep

Write the letter of the best answer choice.

11. Location, shape, and elevation help define Earth's ____.
    A. constructive forces
    B. destructive forces
    C. surface features
    D. sediments

12. Erosion and weathering are examples of ____.
    A. constructive forces
    B. destructive forces
    C. surface features
    D. land buildup

13. Volcanic activity is an example of ____.
    A. erosion
    B. constructive force
    C. weathering
    D. alluvial plain formation

14. Thanks to wind and water, the products of one place's weathering become materials for another place's ____.
    A. volcanoes
    B. glacial till
    C. coral reefs
    D. deposition

Inquiry Skills

15. Make a Model Suppose you have a lump of sugar, water, a spray bottle, and a cake pan. Describe how you could use those items to construct a working model of erosion and deposition.

16. Infer The icy sidewalk in front of your school was treated with salt to help the ice melt. In the spring, you noticed the cement was crumbly and falling apart. What type of weathering did you observe? Explain.

Map the Concept

Complete the concept map using words from the list below. Some words belong in more than one category.

glaciers **acids** **weathering** **erosion** **deposition** **volcanoes** **sediments** **continental shelf** **plateau** **lava**

Destructive Forces	Surface Features	Constructive Forces

Critical Thinking

17. Apply What features on the ocean floor are similar to features on Earth's surface?

18. Synthesize Formations called stalactites and stalagmites grow in caves where the water evaporates. A mineral deposit, calcium carbonate, is left behind. Describe another location in nature where a similar process takes place.

19. Apply Look at the photograph of the meandering river on page C25. Water flows at different speeds through a meander. Where do you think the water flows the fastest? Explain your reasoning.

20. Evaluate Two statues were put up in the center of a busy industrial city. One is made from marble and the other is made from granite. Predict what the statues may look like 50 years from now. Explain your reasoning.

Performance Assessment

Draw a Map

Illustrate four of the following terms with a drawing. Your drawing should accurately represent the main characteristics of these features.

continental slope — continental shelf — continental rise

barrier island — seamount — ocean

shoreline — marsh/swamp — sand dune

beach — sand — mid-ocean ridge

Earth's Structure

Lesson Preview

LESSON
1

Cool and crusty on the outside, hot on the inside—what is Earth's structure like?

Read about it in Lesson 1.

LESSON
2

Shaking earthquakes and erupting volcanoes—what forces of nature cause these dramatic events to occur?

Read about them in Lesson 2.

LESSON
3

Some mountains are tall and jagged. Others are rounded and covered in trees. How do mountains form?

Read about it in Lesson 3.

Lesson 1

What Is Earth's Structure?

Why It Matters...

Earth has a layered structure, with solid rock at the surface and partly liquid rock material below. Understanding Earth's structure can help scientists predict when a geyser or volcano will erupt, or how a river will change course over time.

PREPARE TO INVESTIGATE

Inquiry Skill

Use Models When you use models, you study, make, or operate something that stands for a real-world process or action. Models can help you to understand better or show how a process or action works.

Materials

- modeling clay, 2 colors
- a small marble
- metric measuring tape
- aluminum foil
- plastic knife

Science and Math Toolbox

For step 4, review **Using a Tape Measure** on page H6.

Investigate

A Model World

Procedure

1. **Collaborate** Working with a partner, roll modeling clay into two balls of different colors. Make one the size of a golf ball and the other the size of a baseball.

2. **Use models** The smaller clay ball represents Earth's outer core. The marble represents its inner core. Push the marble into the center of the smaller clay ball and reshape the clay around it. You now have a model of Earth's two-part core.

3. **Observe** The larger clay ball represents Earth's mantle. Using the plastic knife, cut this clay ball in half. Reshape the clay so that this ball can be wrapped around the two-part core. You now have a model of Earth's core and mantle.

4. **Measure** Use a measuring tape to find the distance around your model at its "equator." Cut a rectangle of foil equal to that distance in length and one-third of that distance in width. Wrap the foil around the mantle and smooth it out. This thin layer of foil represents Earth's crust.

STEP 1

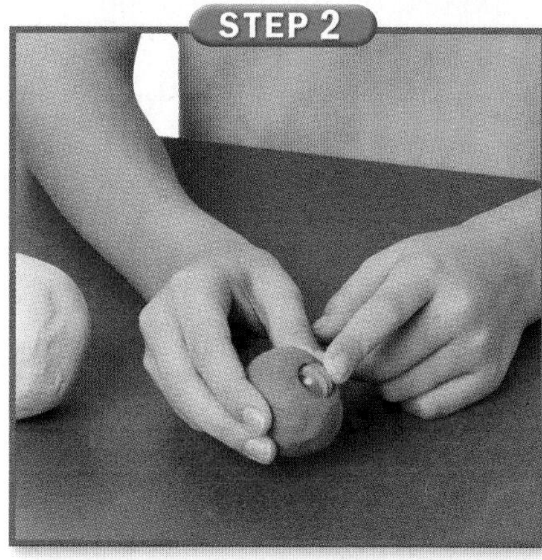
STEP 2

STEP 4

Conclusion

1. **Use Models** In your *Science Notebook*, draw what your model of Earth would look like if you could slice it in half. Label the layers.

2. **Infer** How would you describe the layers that make up Earth's structure? Write about them in your *Science Notebook*.

Investigate More!

Design an Experiment
List some materials you could use to model Earth's layered structure. Describe how you would arrange them.

Learn by Reading

Earth's Structure

VOCABULARY

core	p. C41
crust	p. C40
lithosphere	p. C41
mantle	p. C41
plate tectonics	p. C42

READING SKILL

Text Structure Outline the text on this page using an outline form. Select key words and phrases as topic headings.

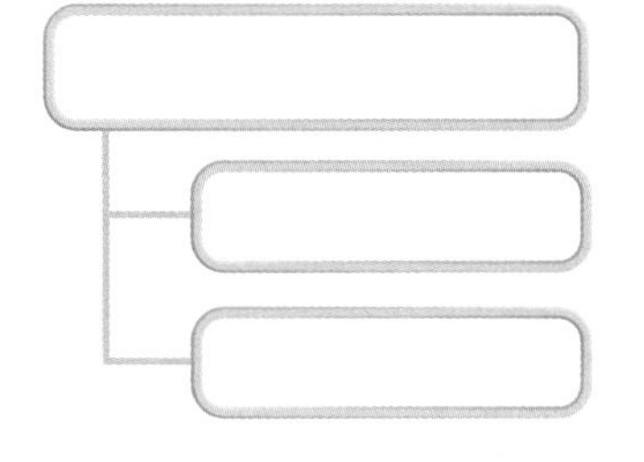

MAIN IDEA **Earth has a layered structure. Its outer layer is made up of moving plates.**

Hot Inside

In many parts of the world, columns of steaming hot water can be found shooting up from Earth's surface. These boiling fountains are known as geysers. Geysers form in places where water drains down a deep channel in Earth's surface. At the bottom of the channel, hot rocks heat the water until steam forms, pushing boiling water up onto the surface. Finally, the built-up pressure forces the remaining water to erupt in a sudden explosion. The existence of geysers suggests that Earth is extremely hot inside.

Yellowstone National Park in Wyoming is well known for its numerous geysers and hot springs. Long before this region became a tourist attraction, Jim Bridger explored its wonders. Bridger was a fur trader, scout, and mountain man. He told everyone he met about the many geysers and amazing sights of the region.

Visit Yellowstone today, and you too can see evidence of Earth's hot interior. But just how hot is it inside Earth?

"Geysers spout up 70 feet, with a terrible hissing noise, at regular intervals. In this section are the great springs, so hot that meat is readily cooked in them...."

Jim Bridger (1804–1881)
Geyser Gazer

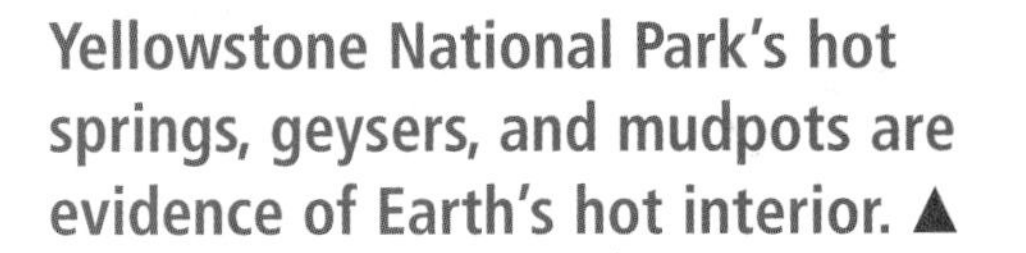

Yellowstone National Park's hot springs, geysers, and mudpots are evidence of Earth's hot interior. ▲

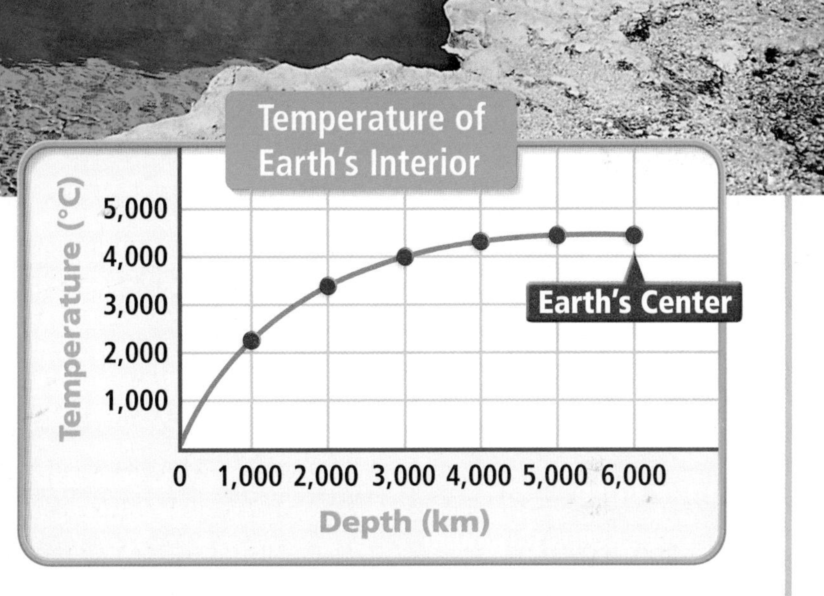

Earth's temperature increases about 25°C per km in the crust, then more gradually from the upper mantle to its center. ▶

Scientists cannot travel very far below Earth's surface to measure temperatures directly. By studying mines and holes drilled in the crust, scientists know that the temperature increases about 2 to 3°C for every 0.1 km (300 ft) below the surface. However, the deepest drill holes reach less than 15 km (9 mi) below the surface. So scientists depend on other, less direct evidence.

Scientists study geysers and volcanic activity to learn what Earth is like inside. They also conduct experiments on surface rocks and minerals under conditions of high pressure and temperature.

More information about Earth's interior can be gained by observing seismic waves. These waves are vibrations that travel through the solid Earth during earthquakes. Seismic waves change as they travel deeper and as they move through different kinds of materials at different temperatures.

TEXT STRUCTURE **What information does the graph on this page present?**

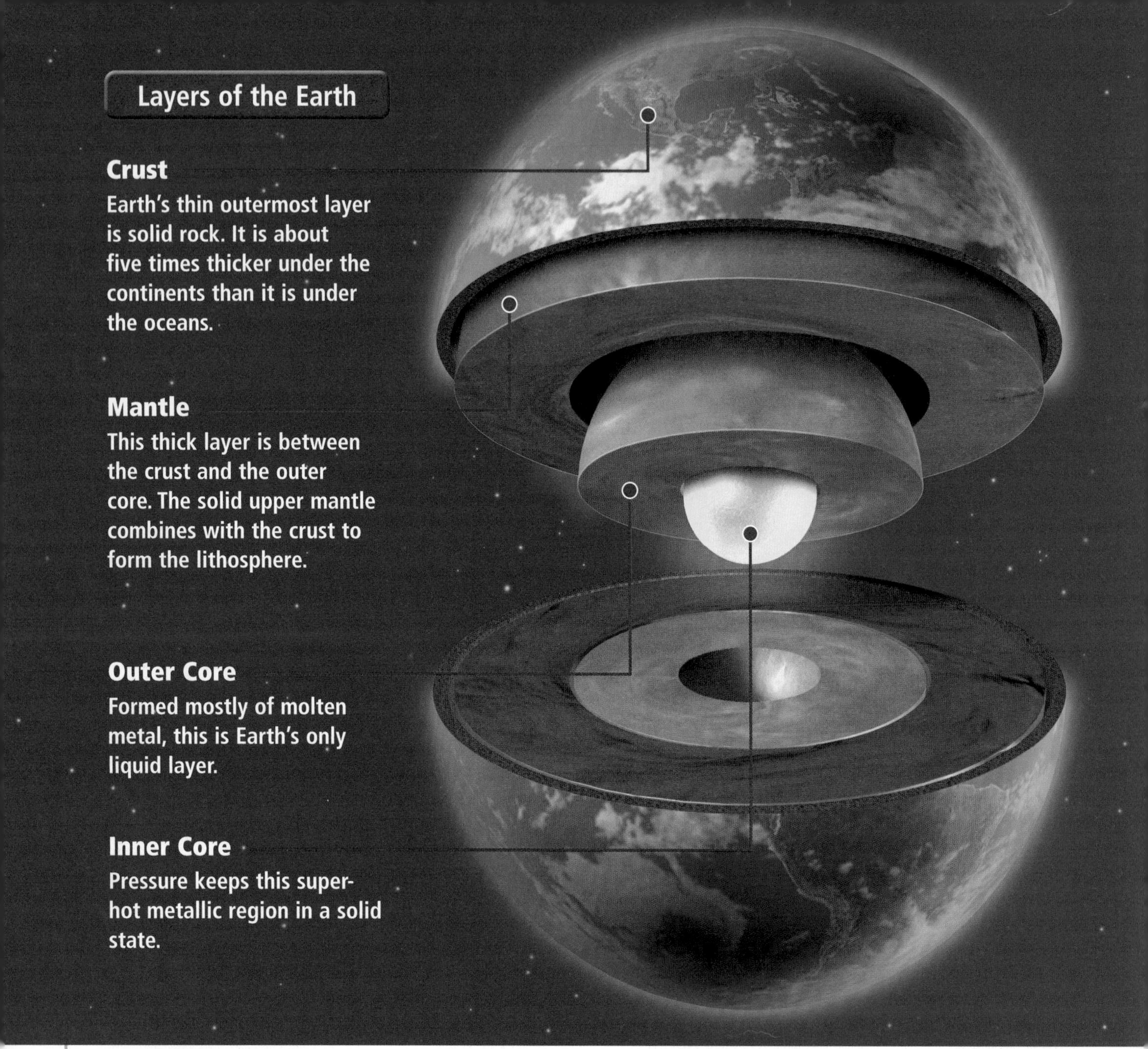

Layers of the Earth

Crust
Earth's thin outermost layer is solid rock. It is about five times thicker under the continents than it is under the oceans.

Mantle
This thick layer is between the crust and the outer core. The solid upper mantle combines with the crust to form the lithosphere.

Outer Core
Formed mostly of molten metal, this is Earth's only liquid layer.

Inner Core
Pressure keeps this super-hot metallic region in a solid state.

Earth's Layers

Earth has a layered structure. Most of these layers are made up of solid or partly melted rock. The innermost layers are mostly a mixture of metals.

Earth's layers vary in thickness. The **crust,** the uppermost layer, is much thinner than the other layers. The crust is nearly all solid rock. Under the continents, the crust is mostly granite and other light rocks. Below the oceans, the crust is mostly made of basalt—a dark, dense rock.

The crust is by far the thinnest of Earth's layers. Under the continents, the average thickness of the crust is about 40 km (24 mi), but it may be as much as 70 km (42 mi) in mountainous regions. The crust is even thinner under the oceans. The ocean-floor crust has a thickness of about 7 km (4 mi).

As discussed earlier, temperature increases as you go deeper into the Earth. So, the deeper that rocks are located, the hotter they are.

The layer just below Earth's crust is the **mantle.** The mantle is about 2,900 km (1,800 mi) thick and makes up more than two-thirds of Earth's mass. At the boundary where the upper mantle meets the crust, the mantle rock is solid. This solid upper mantle and crust combine to form a rigid shell called the **lithosphere.**

Below the lithosphere, much of the rock material in the mantle is partially melted. This material can flow very slowly, like plastic that has been heated almost to its melting point. The solid lithosphere can be thought of as "floating" on this thick lower mantle.

The innermost of Earth's layers is the **core,** which extends to the center of the Earth. The core is divided into two regions, or layers—the outer core and the inner core. The outer core is about 2,200 km (1,400 mi) thick, and is the only layer that is in a liquid state. It is made up mostly of molten iron and nickel, with some sulfur and oxygen also present.

The inner core, about 1,200 km (720 mi) thick, is even hotter than the outer core. It is probably made up of iron and nickel as well. However, the extremely high pressure so deep inside Earth keeps this metal from melting.

When a peach is used as a model of Earth, what does the peach pit represent? ▶

Many scientists believe that the presence of molten iron and nickel in Earth's core explains why Earth is surrounded by a magnetic field. According to one theory, convection currents move slowly throughout the liquid outer core. Electric currents are produced as Earth rotates, setting up Earth's magnetic field.

A hard-boiled egg is often used to model Earth's structure. The hard, thin shell of the egg is the crust. The egg white is the mantle, and the yolk is the core. Others compare Earth to a peach or similar fruit with a thin skin and a pit in the center.

TEXT STRUCTURE **Use an outline form to organize the information about Earth's layered structure.**

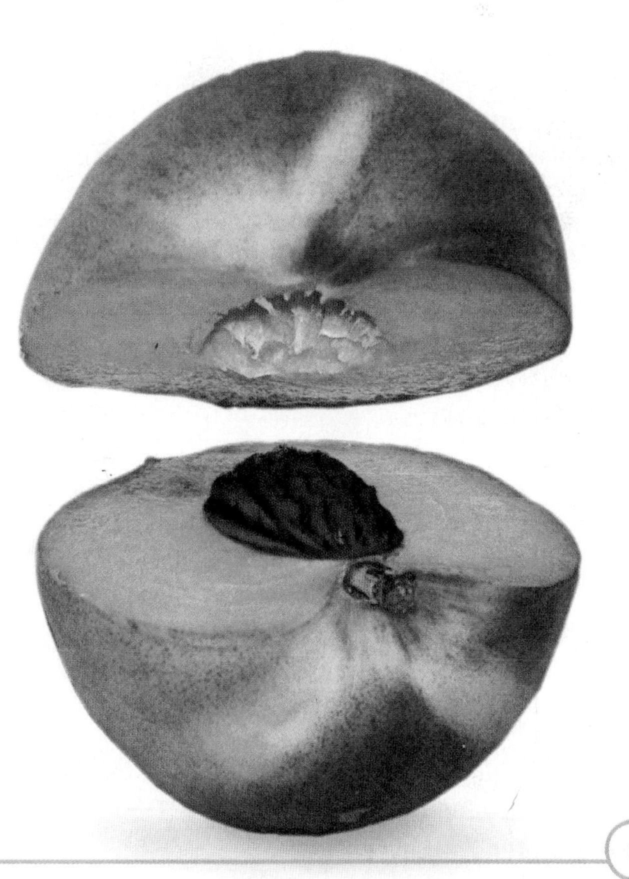

Moving Plates

Have you ever wondered if Earth's surface always looked as it does today? Alfred Wegener wondered. Wegener was a German meteorologist and geologist. In 1915, he suggested that the continents were moving very slowly across Earth's surface.

Known as the theory of continental drift, Wegener's ideas were based on evidence that included fossils and rock formations. However, he could not explain how the continents could move through the solid crust of the sea floor or what force could move them. So, his theory was rejected by most scientists.

In the 1950s, scientists discovered that molten rock from the mantle was rising to Earth's surface in the ocean basins. As this rock cooled and hardened, it was being added to Earth's crust.

This discovery led scientists to suggest that the lithosphere is not one solid shell of rock. In fact, they now believe that the lithosphere is broken up into giant slabs of rock called plates. These plates seem to "float" on top of the mantle, much like giant ships floating on a sea of thick molten rock.

The idea of giant plates of rock moving slowly across Earth's surface is called **plate tectonics.** As you might expect, the plates move very slowly. Their average speed is about 10 cm (4 in.) a year. However, over millions of years, plates can move thousands of kilometers.

There are two kinds of plates. Oceanic plates consist almost entirely of dense ocean-floor material. Continental plates are made up of lighter continental rock "riding" on top of denser rock.

This map shows Earth's major plates. Plates interact along their boundaries. ▼

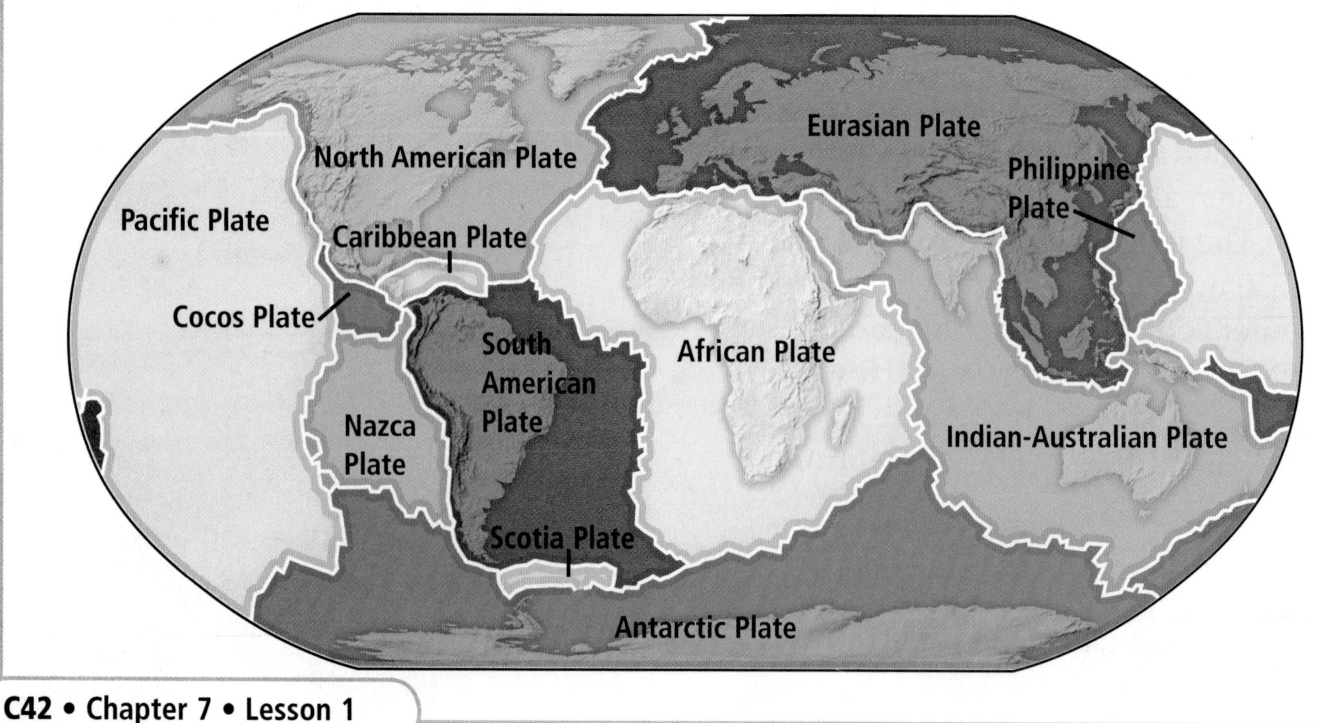

Plates interact at their edges, or plate boundaries. The pictures show the interaction that takes place at each type of boundary.

At converging boundaries, two plates converge, or move toward each other. Eventually they collide. When plates collide, one may ride up over the other. The upper plate forces the edge of the lower plate under the surface. This is called subduction.

Subduction usually occurs when a continental plate and an oceanic plate converge. The dense rock of the oceanic plate slides under the lighter rock of the continental plate.

At diverging boundaries, two plates move away, or diverge, from each other. Molten rock rises up in the gap between the plates, forming new crust. This usually happens in the middle of the ocean floor, so it is called sea-floor spreading.

In some places, plates simply slide past each other in opposite directions. These are known as sliding boundaries. Whether converging, diverging, or sliding, Earth's plates never stop moving and changing. New rock is added to Earth's crust in some places, while old rock is "lost" to the mantle in other places.

The moving, separating, and merging of the continents has been happening for billions of years. You can learn more about plate tectonics in the Readers' Theater feature on pages C46–C49.

TEXT STRUCTURE **Describe three ways in which Earth's plates interact at their boundaries.**

Types of Plate Boundaries

ocean trench

Converging Boundaries

Two plates move toward each other. One plate may move under the other in a process called subduction.

Diverging Boundaries

Two plates move away from each other. Molten rock rises to fill the gap, creating new crust.

Sliding Boundaries

Two plates slide past each other, moving in opposite directions.

◀ A fossil of a tropical fern like the one shown below was found here. Since the fossil formed, the region is believed to have moved 3,200 km (2,000 mi) on a section of a continental plate.

Evidence for Moving Plates

Scientists conclude that Earth's plates have been moving for at least two billion years. They base this conclusion on evidence found in rocks at Earth's surface. These rocks have been eroded and deposited since the planet first took shape.

As you learned in Chapter 6, all rock at Earth's surface is subject to weathering and erosion. Weathered rock, or sediment, is deposited in layers. In turn, the layers eventually change into sedimentary rocks.

Layers of sedimentary rocks provide clues to changes that were taking place at the time the layers were forming. For example, the layers can show the mineral content of the rocks and how the sediment was deposited. The layers may also contain fossils.

A **fossil** is the physical remains or traces of a plant or animal that lived long ago. Fossils are usually found in layers of sedimentary rock.

By studying fossils in rock layers, scientists can get an idea of how plates moved in Earth's past. For example, fossils of similar species have been discovered on opposite sides of an ocean along the edges of different continents. Scientists believe that the fossils come from a period when those continents were joined. Over time, the continents separated, taking the fossils to new locations.

Some fossils seem to be very far from where they were deposited. Fossils of tropical plants and animals have been found in polar regions. Fossils of fish have been found near the tops of mountains. Scientists believe that the fossils were carried to their present locations by the movement of tectonic plates.

TEXT STRUCTURE **Use an outline form to organize information about the evidence supporting the idea of moving plates.**

Lesson Wrap-Up

Visual Summary

Earth has a layered structure consisting of the crust, mantle, outer core, and inner core.

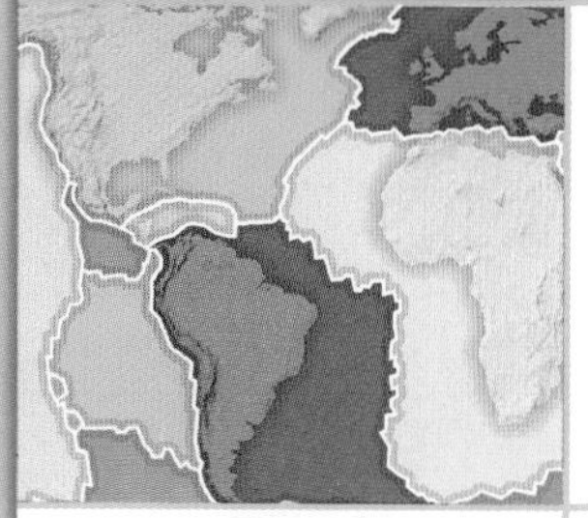

The crust and upper mantle make up the rigid lithosphere, which is broken into large sections called plates.

Plates interact in three ways at their boundaries: they may converge, diverge, or slide past one another.

Fossils and other material in layers of rock provide evidence of Earth's moving plates.

MATH **Calculate Diameter** Earth's inner and outer core combined are about the size of Mars. Using the measurements on page C41, calculate the diameter of Mars in kilometers.

ART **Build a Sculpture** Build a movable sculpture that models one or more plate boundaries. Use modeling clay, fabric, or other available materials. Write a paragraph that explains what the model shows.

Review

1. **MAIN IDEA** What parts of a hard-boiled egg are used to model Earth's structure?

2. **VOCABULARY** What parts of Earth's structure combine to form the lithosphere?

3. **READING SKILL: Text Structure** Outline the text under the head "Moving Plates" on page C42.

4. **CRITICAL THINKING: Applying** At a converging boundary, why do ocean plates usually subduct beneath continental plates?

5. **INQUIRY SKILL: Use Models** Describe how you would use small rocks, pieces of board, and a tub of water to model Earth's lithosphere.

TEST PREP

The thinnest layer of Earth's structure is the

A. crust.

B. lithosphere.

C. inner core.

D. mantle.

Technology

Visit **www.eduplace.com/scp/** to find out more about Earth's structure.

Alfred Wegener and Pangaea

What is Pangaea? Scientist Alfred Wegener (1880–1930) believed that long ago the seven continents were joined together, forming a supercontinent he called Pangaea.

Characters

Alfred Wegener

The Seven Continents:
Africa, Antarctica, Asia, Australia, Europe, North America, South America

The setting is planet Earth, and Wegener is taking the stage.

Wegener *(to audience)*: Good afternoon. I am German scientist Alfred Wegener.

Europe *(aside)*: His name is pronounced "VAY-guh-ner."

Wegener: My friends and I are here to present my theory of continental drift, which I published in the year 1915.

North America *(shocked)*: Did you say "continental drift?" Are you suggesting that continents move?

Wegener: Don't act so surprised! Surely you know that continents move during earthquakes and volcanic eruptions.

North America: Yes, but—

Wegener *(holding up one hand at North America)*: Let me tell you my story. Then you will understand. It all started when I was a young man fascinated by maps. One day I noticed that the coasts of two continents appear to fit together, like pieces of a jigsaw puzzle. Africa and South America, will you demonstrate?

Africa *(moving toward South America)*: If I turn a little this way, and South America rotates that way . . .

South America: Yes, we *could* fit together, couldn't we?

Wegener: Yes! That got me thinking. I found out that nearly identical fossils have been discovered on both sides of the Atlantic Ocean, as well as identical rock layers. There are similar pairs of mountain ranges, too, such as the Scottish Highlands in Europe and the Appalachians in North America.

Asia: What are you driving at? Are you saying that some of the continents were once joined together?

Wegener: Not *some* of the continents—*all* of the continents! That's my theory.

Antarctica: Incredible!

Wegener: Isn't it? I call this joined continent *Pangaea.* That's Greek for "all the Earth." Might the seven of you demonstrate what Pangaea looked like?

Wegener waves directions. The continents move together to form Pangaea.

Australia *(stumbling)*: This is terribly disorienting. Am I still Down Under?

South America: Hey, someone's stepping on my Galápagos Islands!

Antarctica: It's getting a bit too warm around here.

Wegener: Stop right there! Perfect! As you can see, the continents fit together into one supercontinent. According to my theory, this is how Earth looked about 200 million years ago.

Continental Drift

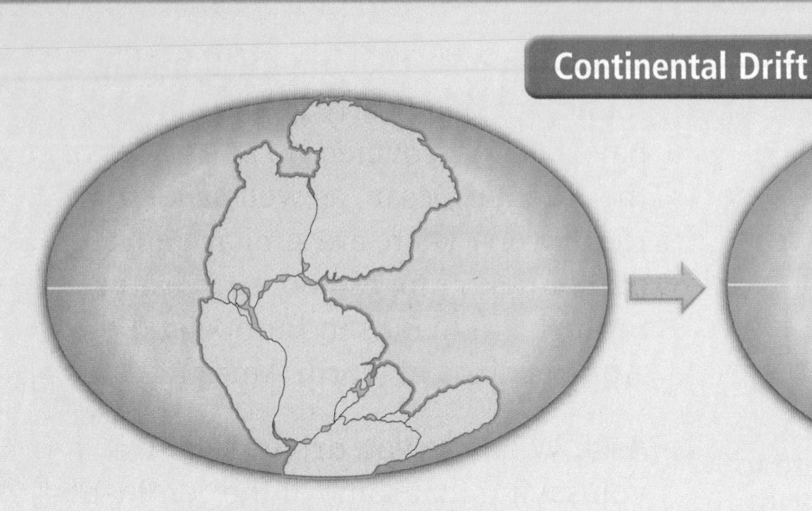

Africa: So animals could wander from me to South America, is that right?

South America: Plant seeds could travel easily, too.

Wegener: Right and right. But over the years, slowly but surely, the continents drifted apart.

Wegner gestures at the continents. They drift apart, back to their modern-day positions.

Australia: Well, it was fun while it lasted!

Europe *(to the others)*: Maybe I'll see you again in another 200 million years or so.

Wegener: Perhaps, perhaps. My theory about Pangaea explains a great deal about Earth's geography. For example, have you noticed that mountain ranges are found mostly near the edges of continents?

South America: Now that you mention it, I have a rugged mountain range running along my west coast.

North America: That's funny, so do I!

Asia: And I have the Himalayas, that tall mountain range just north of India.

Wegener: According to my theory, mountains arise when continents move into each other. For example, the Himalayas rose when India slammed into the rest of Asia.

Asia: Ouch!

North America: Well, Mr. Wegener, you seem to have solved all the mysteries of our planet. So tell us: Just how *did* continents move around the planet?

Wegener *(shaking his head)*: Well, you've hit upon the weakness of my theory. I could only guess at how the continents moved. Many of my critics enjoyed pointing this out.

100 million years ago

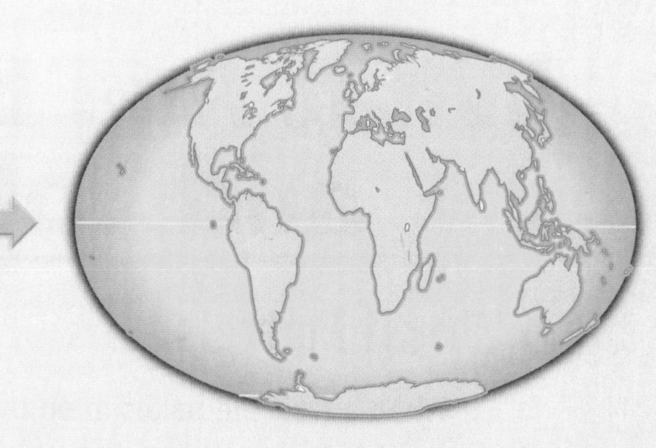
Present Day

Continents gather around Wegener and pat him on the back in consolation.

Wegener: It's okay. After my time, people decided that I was correct. You see, scientists began studying the ocean floor.

Asia: What do oceans have to do with anything?

Wegener: A great deal! Scientists have discovered giant mountain chains, called mid-ocean ridges, in the ocean's depths. In these ridges, molten rocks rise from below Earth's surface and become part of the ocean floor.

Europe: So what does that mean?

Wegener: It means that the ocean floors are moving, too! Oceans and continents move in giant slabs that scientists call tectonic plates. If I'd lived long enough, I would have studied tectonic plates myself.

Australia: I'd like to thank Mr. Wegener for proposing new ideas that challenged old ones. That's very important in science!

Africa: Plus, he used evidence from many different branches of science.

North America: A keen observer and a logical thinker—that's our Mr. Wegener!

Wegener: Why thank you, my friends. I am truly—moved!

All laugh.

Sharing Ideas

1. **READING CHECK** What is Wegener's theory of continental drift?
2. **WRITE ABOUT IT** Describe facts about Earth's geography that Wegener's theory explains.
3. **TALK ABOUT IT** What lessons about science does Wegener's story illustrate?

Lesson 2

What Are Earthquakes and Volcanoes?

Why It Matters...

When a fruit pie bakes in an oven, juices and steam seep up through cracks in the crust. That is similar to how a volcano forms. Volcanic eruptions and earthquakes can be violent events. By learning more about them, people may be able to avoid some of the dangers they represent.

PREPARE TO INVESTIGATE

Inquiry Skill

Analyze Data When you analyze data, you look for patterns in information you collect. Those patterns can lead you to draw conclusions, make predictions, and state generalizations.

Materials

- world atlas
- blank world map
- red pencil
- green pencil

◀ A volcanologist is a scientist who studies volcanoes.

Investigate

Picking a Pattern

Procedure

1. **Compare** Read and compare the lists of earthquake and volcano locations below. What similarities do you find?

Earthquakes	Year
Banda Sea, East Indonesia	1938
Concepción, Chile	1751
Esmeraldas (offshore), Ecuador	1906
Kamchatka Peninsula, Russia	1952
Kobe, Japan	1995
Prince William Sound, Alaska	1964
San Francisco, California	1906
Tangshan, China	1976

Volcanoes	Year
Mt. Pinatubo, Phillippines	1991
Mt. St. Helens, Washington	1980
Krakatau, Indonesia	1883
Mt. Fuji, Japan	1707
Arenal, Costa Rica	1968
Momotombo, Nicaragua	1609
Mt. Hood, Oregon	1865
Tiatia (Kurile Islands), Russia	1973

2. **Use Models** Use an atlas to find the locations of the earthquakes and volcanoes.

3. **Record Data** Mark each location on the blank world map. Draw a red triangle for a volcano. Draw a green circle for an earthquake. Check your work.

STEP 2

STEP 3

Conclusion

1. **Analyze Data** In your *Science Notebook,* draw conclusions about the pattern you see.
2. **Predict** Using what you know about Earth's structure, predict the relationship between the planet's plates and the places where most volcanoes and earthquakes occur.

Investigate More!

Research Use the Internet or other reference sources to research a recent major earthquake or volcanic eruption. Where did it take place? What damage did it cause? Report your findings.

Learn by Reading

Earthquakes and Volcanoes

VOCABULARY

earthquake	p. C54
epicenter	p. C54
fault	p. C52
focus	p. C54
magma	p. C56
seismic waves	p. C53

READING SKILL

Cause and Effect Track the general causes and effects of faulting.

MAIN IDEA **Earthquakes and volcanoes change Earth's surface, usually at plate boundaries.**

At the Faults

As you have learned, Earth's crust moves very slowly. Typically, this motion can hardly be felt. But at times, it can cause sudden and unexpected changes to Earth's surface.

Most major surface changes occur at or near plate boundaries. Recall from the last lesson that plates may push together (converge), move apart (diverge), or slide past each other at plate boundaries.

Faults are cracks in Earth's crust along which movement takes place. At a fault, rocks often bend and fold. Sometimes, they lock together and jam along the fault. Over many years, stress builds up on the rocks as the plates strain against each other. Finally, the rocks break. The plates shudder and jolt into a new position. This sudden movement causes Earth's crust to shake.

▼ The San Andreas fault extends almost the full length of California.

The wavy lines from a seismograph indicate the strength of seismic waves moving through Earth's crust. ▼

As the crust shakes, it sends out shock waves of energy known as **seismic waves.** A seismograph has sensors that detect and measure vibrations of Earth's crust. The seismograph produces a record of seismic waves called a seismogram.

The movement of rocks along a fault is called faulting. During faulting, the rocks crack or split into blocks. The blocks then continue to move in relation to each other, sometimes leading to further faulting.

The drawings show the three main types of faults. Each is caused by a different type of force applied in the region where movement takes place.

At diverging boundaries, the force stretches rock. Eventually the rock breaks and one block moves down along a sloping crack. Mid-ocean ridges are typical locations for these types of faults.

Other faults occur at converging boundaries. Here, the force squeezes rock. When the rock breaks, one block moves up along a sloping crack while the other moves down. Often this occurs in regions of subduction, where one plate plunges below the other.

The third type of fault occurs in regions where blocks move horizontally past each other. These faults are common at sliding boundaries, such as the San Andreas Fault in California.

CAUSE AND EFFECT **What happens when stress builds up along a fault?**

Different Kinds of Faults

Fault at Diverging Boundary
As sections of the crust move apart, rocks are stretched until they snap, causing one block to move down along a sloping crack.

Fault at Converging Boundary
Rocks are compressed as they come together, causing one block to move up along a sloping crack as the other moves down.

Fault at Sliding Boundary
Rocks grind against each other as they move horizontally past each other in opposite directions. Pressure builds up along the fault until the rocks break.

▲ The city of Taipei in Taiwan suffered a devastating earthquake on September 21, 1999.

Earthquakes

An **earthquake** is a violent shaking of Earth's crust. The release of built-up energy along a fault is what makes Earth shake, or quake. The energy released depends on how much rock breaks and how far the blocks of rock shift.

With the records produced by seismographs, scientists can measure an earthquake's energy. This measurement expresses its size, or magnitude, using a scale called the Richter scale. For example, an earthquake with a magnitude of less than 3.5 may not even be felt, although it is recorded by the seismograph. An earthquake measuring 7.5 is a major earthquake.

The surface effects, or intensity, of an earthquake vary from place to place. Intensity is measured by what can be seen and felt on the surface.

What people see and feel often depends on how far they are from the earthquake's focus. The **focus** of an earthquake is the point underground where the faulting occurs. Most focus points are less than 72 km (45 mi) below Earth's surface.

The point on the surface directly above the focus is an earthquake's **epicenter.** That is where the intensity is strongest. Why? The epicenter is the closest point to the focus, where seismic waves are strongest.

The shaking is caused by the energy of the seismic waves. Long after the initial earthquake occurs, continued seismic wave activity can cause miniquakes, or aftershocks.

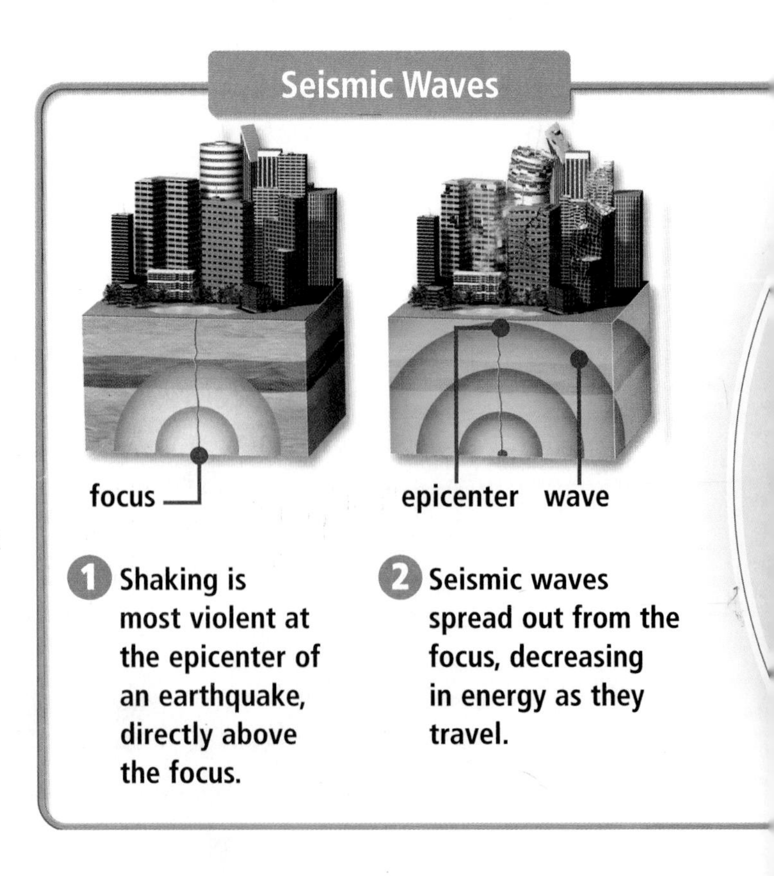

There are two general types of seismic waves—body waves and surface waves. Waves that travel through Earth's interior are called body waves. The deeper they extend, the faster they travel.

Body waves called P waves can travel through Earth's interior in less than an hour. They can pass through solid and liquids. As P waves pass into and out of the liquid outer core, they change direction. They return to Earth's surface, where they cause back-and-forth motions of rock.

Body waves called S waves travel slightly slower than P waves. When S waves reach the surface, they cause it to move up and down. However, S waves can travel only through solids. So, S waves that pass from the mantle into the liquid outer core lose their energy and do not return to the surface.

Surface waves, or L waves, travel along Earth's surface. These waves travel more slowly than body waves. Surface waves do not travel too far from the epicenter of an earthquake. However, surface waves cause the most damage, because they make the ground swell and roll like ocean waves.

The damage caused by surface waves can be extensive. Buildings fall down and roads heave up. Bridges collapse. Glass breaks. Rivers change course or flood their banks. Trees topple and cliffs crumble. Out at sea, massive waves are set in motion. These waves, often 30 m high (90 ft), can reach speeds of 500 km/h (300 mi/h). Such waves can cause great amounts of damage when they crash onshore.

CAUSE AND EFFECT **Why do surface waves cause great damage?**

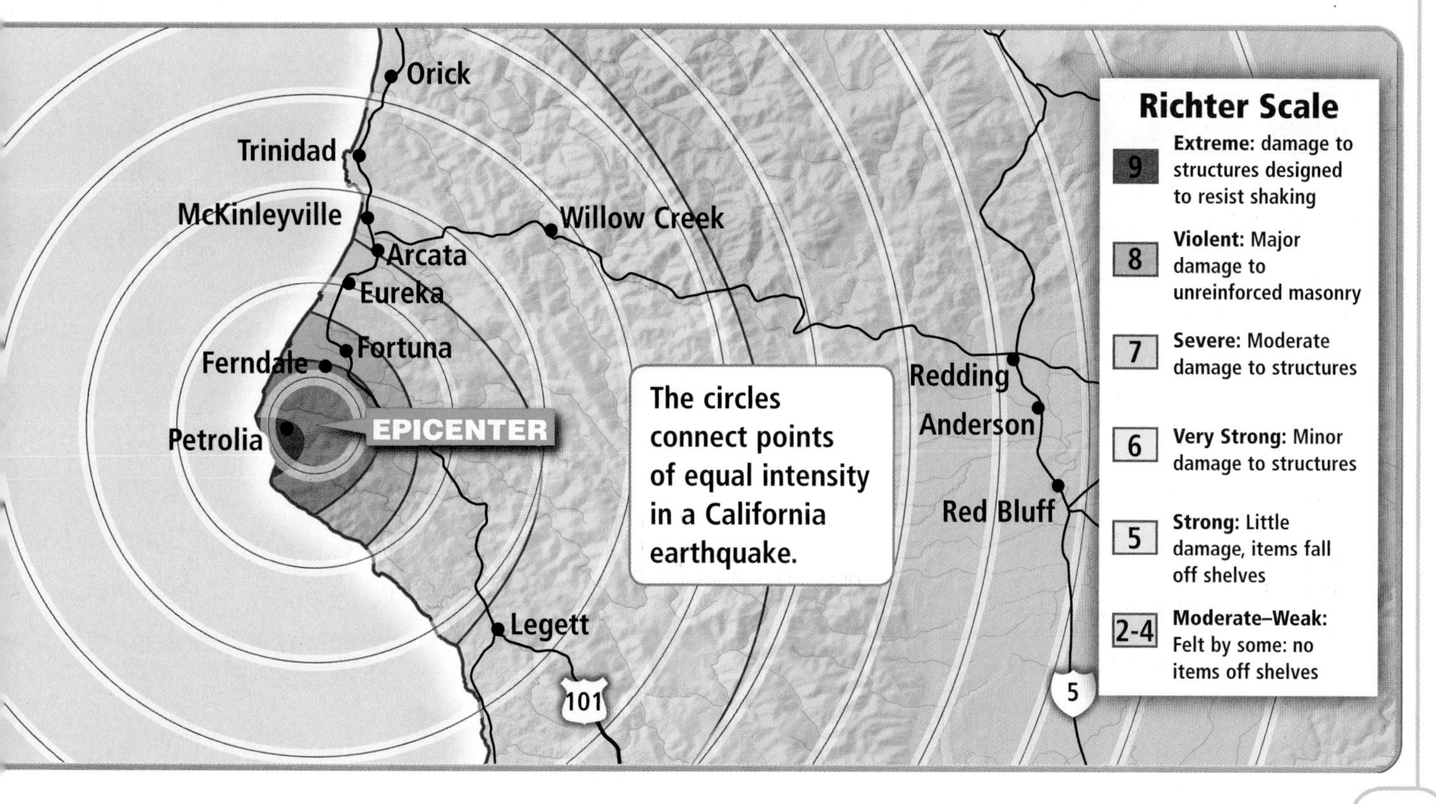

The circles connect points of equal intensity in a California earthquake.

Volcanoes

A volcano is an opening in Earth's surface through which melted rock, hot gases, rock fragments, and ash burst forth, or erupt. A violent eruption can release rivers of red-hot molten rock, hissing jets of poisonous gas, curling clouds of thick gray ash, and explosions of scorched rock.

You can see why volcanoes are sometimes referred to as mountains of fire. In fact, the word *volcano* comes from the ancient Roman god of fire, Vulcan.

How do such mountains of fire form? Volcanoes come from Earth's hot interior. Most volcanoes start 37 to 100 miles below the surface. At these depths, rock can become so hot it melts. Melted rock below Earth's surface is called **magma.**

When rock melts, it releases gases. These gases mix with the magma, making it lighter than the solid rock around it. Slowly, the gas-filled magma rises toward the surface. As it rises, it melts rock around it, gradually forming a large chamber. This chamber may be only a few kilometers below the surface.

Under pressure from the weight of surrounding rock, the magma is forced to find an escape. It melts or forces a channel into weak or cracked rock. Within this channel, it pushes upward. Once near the surface, gas and magma burst through a central opening, or vent. The erupting material builds up, forming a volcanic mountain, or volcano.

After an eruption, a volcano usually collapses into a bowl-shaped mouth called a crater. At the bottom of the crater lies the central vent. Many volcanoes have repeated eruptions. In these later eruptions, some of the volcanic material in the channel may remain below the surface. It may also push out through side vents.

Lava Flows
Volcanoes have been called mountains of fire.

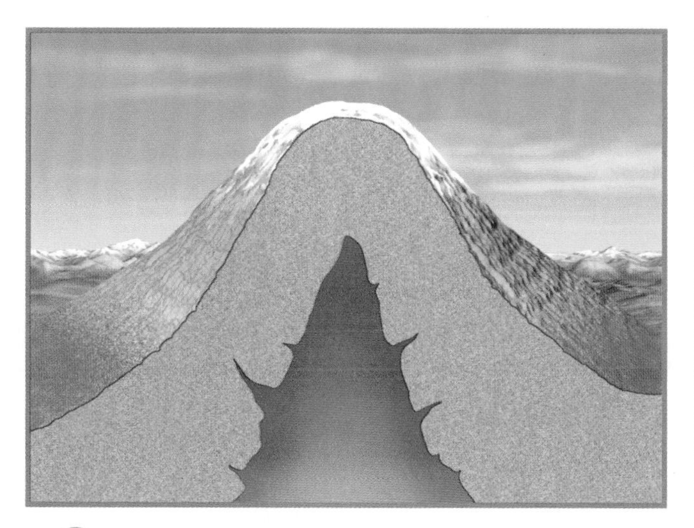

1 Hot, gas-filled magma rises, melting rock along the way, until it forms a chamber near the surface.

2 Pressure builds until the gas and magma force open a channel leading to the surface. Volcanic material moves through this channel and erupts through the vent.

Three main types of volcanic material are ejected during an eruption. The main one, magma, is called lava once it reaches the surface. It may be fast-flowing and liquid-like or thick and slow-flowing.

As it comes from a volcano, flowing lava may be hotter than 1,100°C (2,000°F). As it cools, lava hardens into formations such as boulders, domes, cones, tubes, and smooth or jagged sheets.

Rock fragments may form when gas in sticky magma cannot escape. Pressure builds up until the gas blasts the magma apart.

The fragments erupt into dust, ash, and large chunks called bombs. Small bombs, called cinders, may be no larger than a baseball. The largest bombs can be more than 1 m (3 ft) wide and weigh 100 tons!

Gases are also released during a volcanic eruption. Mostly steam, volcanic gases often contain poisonous chemicals. These gases mix with ash to form a deadly black smoke.

There are different classes of volcanoes and volcanic cones. Shield volcanoes form when a lot of lava flows smoothly from a vent and spreads out to cover a wide area. This action creates a broad, low, dome-shaped volcano.

Cinder cones form when mostly rock fragments erupt and are deposited around the vent. This creates a cone-shaped volcano with steep sides.

Composite volcanoes are also cone shaped. The sides of these volcanoes are steeper than those of a shield cone, but not as steep as a cinder cone.

CAUSE AND EFFECT **What causes magma to rise to the surface?**

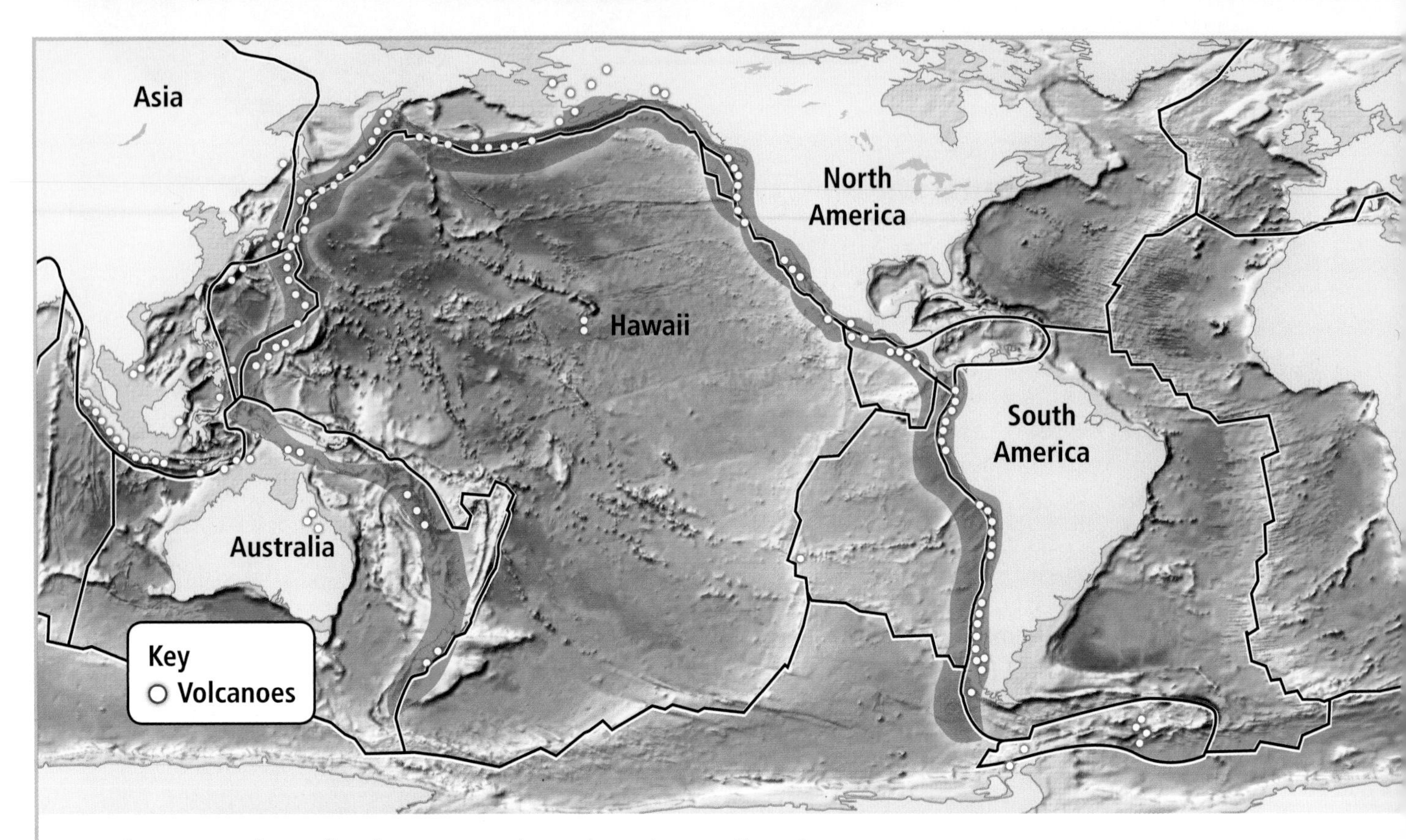

A large number of volcanoes and earthquakes strike along the edge of the Pacific Ocean. This explains why this zone is called the Ring of Fire. ▲

Ring of Fire

Many earthquakes and volcanoes occur in a zone that borders the Pacific Ocean. For that reason, this zone has been named the Ring of Fire.

The Ring of Fire outlines Earth's subduction zones, places where one of Earth's plates is forced under another. The Pacific Plate converges with several continental plates to form the Ring of Fire.

Faulting during subduction causes earthquakes and can also lead to volcanic activity. As the subducting plate sinks into the mantle, it melts to form magma. The magma may later rise to the surface as a line of volcanoes.

On the ocean floor, a deep narrow valley called an ocean trench may form along a subduction zone. Resulting volcanoes often parallel the trench, usually in an arc.

Faulting at diverging boundaries also causes earthquakes and creates volcanoes. Diverging boundaries are usually located near the middle of ocean basins. At these boundaries, magma rises to the surface between separating plates, creating volcanic mountain ranges known as ocean ridges. Faulting at the ridges leads to earthquakes.

CAUSE AND EFFECT **Why is the Pacific rim a region of earthquakes and active volcanoes?**

Lesson Wrap-Up

Visual Summary

An earthquake is a violent shaking of Earth's crust caused by faulting, which shifts rock and sends out seismic waves.

Volcanoes form when gas-filled magma rises through Earth's interior. This forces volcanic materials to burst through a vent.

Many volcanoes and earthquakes occur in a subduction zone around the Pacific Ocean called the Ring of Fire.

for Home and School

MATH **Make a Graph** Research three recent earthquakes. Make a bar graph that shows the Richter scale readings for each earthquake. Share your graph with the class.

TECHNOLOGY **Prepare a Report** How can old buildings be reinforced to withstand earthquakes? Research this question on the Internet or at the library. Write a report to present your findings.

Review

1. **MAIN IDEA** Why do earthquakes and volcanoes usually occur at plate boundaries?

2. **VOCABULARY** Define *epicenter* and *focus* and describe their relationship.

3. **READING SKILL: Cause and Effect** Describe the cause-and-effect relationship that creates volcanoes in the Ring of Fire.

4. **CRITICAL THINKING: Analyze** How would Earth be different if its crust did not move and it lacked tectonic plates?

5. **INQUIRY SKILL: Analyze Data** Research at least five recent earthquakes or volcanic eruptions. Add them to the list on Page C51. Do the additional data support the conclusions that this lesson presents about earthquakes and volcanoes?

TEST PREP

Seismic waves that cause the most damage are

A. P waves.

B. surface waves.

C. ocean waves.

D. body waves.

Technology

Visit **www.eduplace.com/scp/** to find out more about the most famous volcanic eruptions in recorded history.

Lesson 3

How Do Mountains Form?

Why It Matters...

Have you ever wondered why mountains often form along a coastline? Or why those mountains look like wrinkled land? Understanding how mountains form allows people to understand what Earth's surface was like in the past. It also helps them predict future changes in Earth's surface.

PREPARE TO INVESTIGATE

Inquiry Skill

Observe When you observe, you use your senses to accurately describe things, making sure to distinguish between facts and opinions or guesses.

Materials

- shoebox lid
- scissors
- wax paper
- moist sand
- measuring cup
- goggles

Science and Math Toolbox

For step 2, review **Measurement** on page H16.

Investigate

Make a Mountain!

Procedure

Safety: Be careful when using scissors. Wear goggles for this investigation.

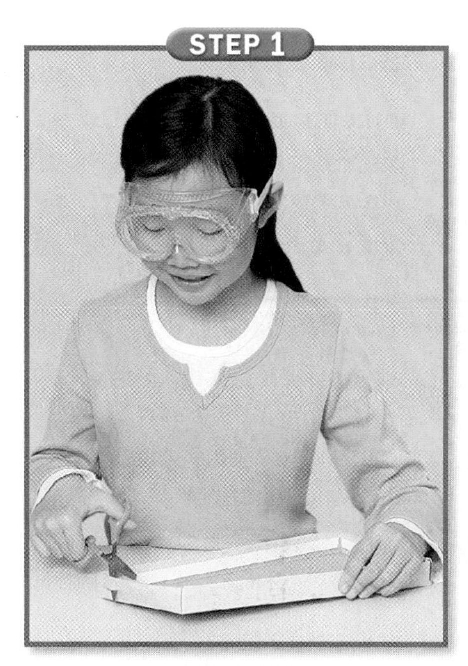
STEP 1

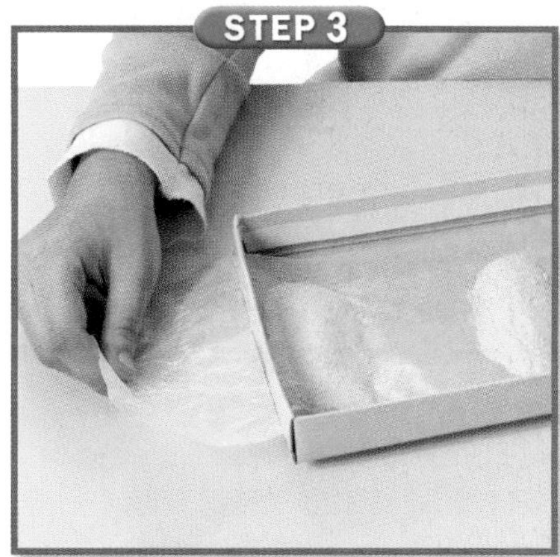
STEP 3

1. **Collaborate** Work with a partner. Place a shoebox lid upside down on a flat surface. Then carefully cut a narrow slit along one end of the lid where it bends up.
2. **Measure** Line the top of the lid with wax paper. It should be the width of the slit and about 2.5 cm (1 in) longer than the lid.
3. **Use Models** Place the wax paper in the lid. Pull one end of the paper about 2.5 cm (1 in) through the slit. Spread half of the sand at the end of the lid near the slit.
4. **Use Models** Spread the other half near the center of the lid. Each pile of sand represents the crust on one of Earth's plates. Draw the model setup in your *Science Notebook*.
5. **Use Models** Slowly pull the wax paper through the slit to model the movement of one of Earth's plates.

Conclusion

1. **Observe** In your *Science Notebook*, draw what happened to the sand as accurately as you can.
2. **Compare** How does what happened to the sand compare to what happens to rocks in the crust when two plates collide?

Investigate More!

Design an Experiment
Select materials to model what happens along a diverging boundary.

Learn by Reading

Mountain Formation

VOCABULARY

READING SKILL

Categorize/Classify Use a chart to list the types of mountains and the forces that build them.

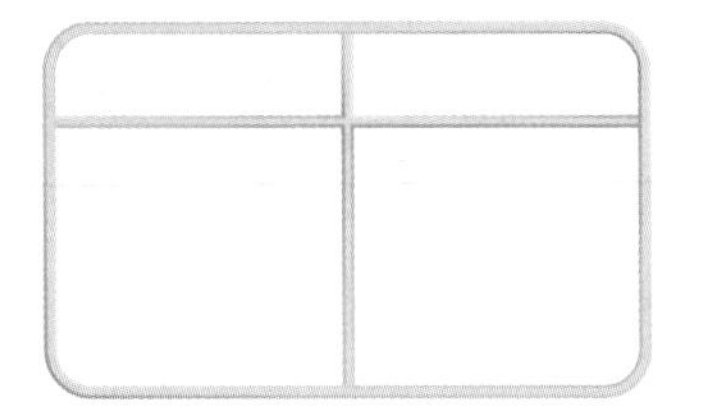

MAIN IDEA Mountains are formed by various processes, usually at plate boundaries. They can be classified by how they form and by their height.

Folding and Faulting Forces

Awesome! That is what you might think as you look down from a high mountain peak or gaze at mountains along a horizon. Indeed, mountains are awe-inspiring. Not only are they Earth's highest surface features, but they are some of its most beautiful. From the Alps in Central Europe to the Rockies in North America, mountains make up the backdrop to many of the world's scenic spots.

Grand in scale and great in mass, mountains may seem permanent. However, like Earth's other surface features, they are continually being created and destroyed.

Most mountains form at or near plate boundaries. In fact, most of the largest mountain ranges form where two plates collide and force layers of rock into folds. These are known as **fold mountains.** The Andes shown below are examples.

Folding
Folding often occurs at the edge of a continent and results in long, narrow mountain ranges, such as the Andes along South America's west coast.

Faulting
Faulting can produce dramatic cliffs when a large section of rock is forced upward or downward, as in this formation in the Rocky Mountains.

Fold mountains often form where an oceanic plate collides with a continental plate. Sediment from the ocean floor becomes attached to the edge of the continent. The sediment and continental rock crumple together, creating rolling folds. As the layers of rock wrinkle, they may also crack. This creates faults, or fractures, in the crust.

Erosion softens the folds over time. For that reason, some of the oldest fold mountains, like Arkansas's Ouachita Mountains, have rounded peaks. These mountains formed before dinosaurs lived!

Fault-block mountains may form wherever faulting occurs. They may even occur at faults within fold mountains. You know that during faulting, rocks break into blocks at a fault. The blocks may move in several ways along one or more faults to create mountains.

Most fault-block mountains appear to form at converging or diverging boundaries. However, mountain-building activity also occurs at sliding faults. The mountains may split and slip sideways like a stack of magazines falling to one side. The new range may then shift along the sliding fault. This is what has happened to some mountain ranges bordering Death Valley in California.

As with fold mountains, erosion helps shape fault-block mountains. Many of the large isolated mountains in the Southwest are fault-block mountains. They are separated by wide plains filled with eroded material from those mountains.

CLASSIFY **Which type of mountain is usually formed at converging boundaries?**

Volcanic Forces

Sometimes volcanic activity forms mountains. This type of mountain usually forms at plate boundaries.

Volcanic activity may happen at converging boundaries when the edge of one plate sinks beneath another and melts into magma. If the magma rises and bursts through the crust, it generally forms a volcanic mountain. This process may even happen within mountains formed by other processes. For example, many of the mountains in the Andes chain in South America are volcanoes.

At diverging boundaries, magma rises up in the gap between the two plates. It then cools on the surface into ridges of new plate material. Recall that mid-ocean ridges form on the ocean floor at diverging boundaries. These underwater mountains make up the world's longest mountain chain.

Volcanic mountains can form away from plate boundaries as well. Magma plumes rising in the mantle create hot spots in the crust. As a plate moves over a hot spot, volcanic material erupts through the plate, creating a chain of volcanic mountains. Sometimes magma rises toward the surface but doesn't break through the crust. It may push up under Earth's crust, creating a dome-shaped mound. The molten rock then cools and hardens. This is how **dome mountains** are formed.

Erosion often continues to shape dome mountains. Irregular peaks and valleys may result. The Black Hills in South Dakota and the Adirondack Mountains in New York are examples of dome mountains.

Some mountains are formed entirely by erosion. The Catskills in New York are an example. These mountains formed when erosion carved out peaks and valleys from a plateau.

CLASSIFY **How are dome mountains different from other mountains?**

hardened magma

Dome

Dome mountains form when volcanic material bulges upward under the crust, hardening as it cools. A number of dome mountains lie to the east of the Rocky Mountain range.

Lesson Wrap-Up

Visual Summary

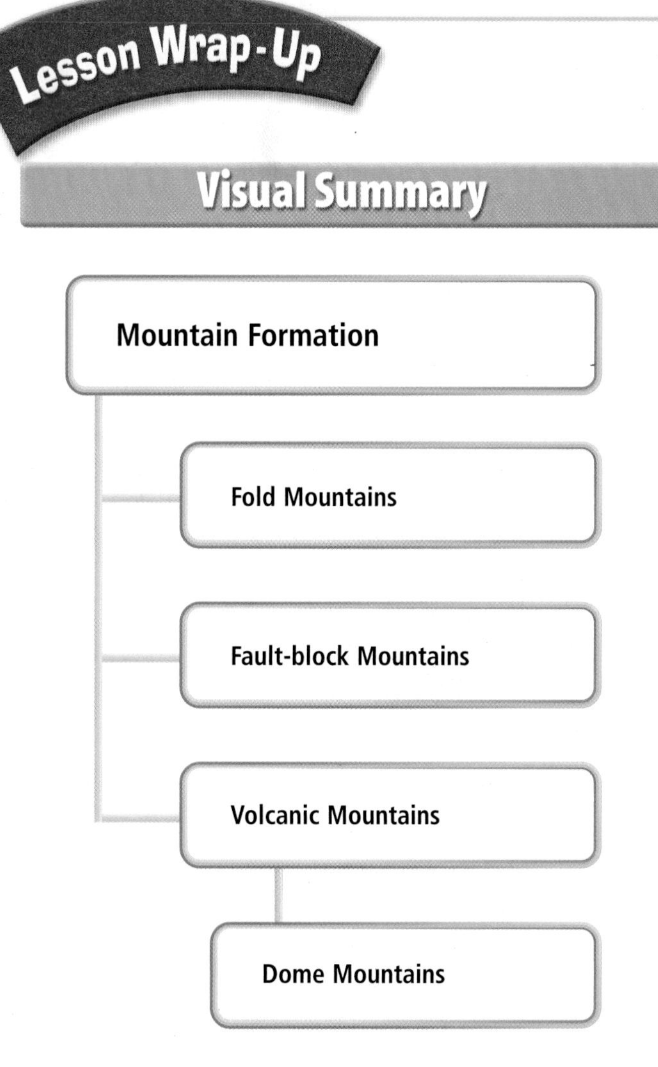

MATH **Convert Units** One of the highest mountains in the Alps is Mont Blanc, which is 4,810 m high. How many kilometers is that?

WRITING **Write a Story** The Navajo in the southwestern United States honor the mountains that surround them. Tibetans honor the Himalayan peak Kang Rimpoche. Choose a culture that lives near mountains and research their beliefs about mountains. Write a story about the people and their mountains.

Review

1. **MAIN IDEA** Name and describe the four types, or classes, of mountains.
2. **VOCABULARY** How does a dome mountain form?
3. **READING SKILL: Categorize/ Classify** Which two types of mountains are formed by volcanic activity?
4. **CRITICAL THINKING: Synthesizing** What might you conclude if you notice sections of warped and wrinkled rock layers on the side of a mountain?
5. **INQUIRY SKILL: Observe** If someone described a dome mountain as "beautiful," would that be an accurate scientific observation? Why or why not?

TEST PREP

Which of these is not a type of mountain?

A. fault-block

B. fold

C. dome

D. diverging

Technology

Visit **www.eduplace.com/scp/** to find out more about mountain formations.

SLEEPING GIANT ERUPTS!

Talk about waking up on the wrong side of the bed! Snow-capped Mount St. Helens slept for a hundred years. Then on May 18, 1980, the volcano blew its top in one of the greatest explosions in recorded history. The sideways blast blew down enough trees to build 300,000 homes. Debris from the volcano was 600 feet deep and even blocked nearby rivers!

Before the eruption, the mountain was 9,677 feet tall. Afterward it was 1,314 feet shorter! Recently, the volcano has shown new signs of activity. Scientists are monitoring it closely to determine if another major eruption will occur.

In 1980, plumes of ash reached a height of 80,000 feet, blocking air traffic. In three days, the ash traveled all the way across the United States.

The View From Inside

This picture is taken from inside the blown-out top of Mount St. Helens. Here you can see the inner walls of the volcano's cone.

steam plume

Danger Mounting **This rising, steaming lump is called a lava dome. As magma pushes up from underneath it rises higher and higher—until the next big eruption. When will it be?**

Chapter 7 Review and Test Prep

Vocabulary

Complete each sentence with a term from the list.

1. The outermost layer of Earth is called the ____.
2. The ____ is composed of the solid upper mantle and the crust.
3. The ____ of an earthquake is the point underground where faulting occurs.
4. The layer of Earth between the crust and the outer core is called the ____.
5. Shock waves of energy released in an earthquake are called ____.
6. The release of energy along a fault causes an ____.
7. Earth's innermost layer is the ____.
8. Molten rock, or ____, that flows on the surface is called lava.
9. A crack in the crust along which rocks move is called a ____.
10. ____ form when magma pushes up from beneath Earth's crust.

core C41
crust C40
dome mountains C64
earthquake C54
epicenter C54
fault C52
fault-block mountains C63
focus C54
fold mountains C62
lithosphere C41
magma C56
mantle C41
seismic waves C53

Test Prep

Write the letter of the best answer choice.

11. Earth's rigid outer layers are broken up into ____.
    A. diverging boundaries
    B. tectonic plates
    C. the crust and the lithosphere
    D. the inner and outer core

12. What instrument measures the strength of an Earthquake?
    A. Thermometer
    B. Anemometer
    C. Spring Scale
    D. Seismograph

13. The temperature of Earth's interior ____.
    A. increases with depth
    B. decreases with depth
    C. is the same throughout
    D. is highest near the equator

14. Where does most mountain formation take place?
    A. at diverging boundaries
    B. at mid-ocean ridges
    C. along ocean trenches
    D. at plate boundaries

Inquiry Skills

15. **Use Models** What kind of fault is shown here? Describe what is happening.

16. **Analyze Data** Describe the information that the Richter scale indicates about an earthquake.

Map the Concept

Complete the concept map using the words listed below.

converging	**Earth**
core	**mantle**
diverging	**sliding**

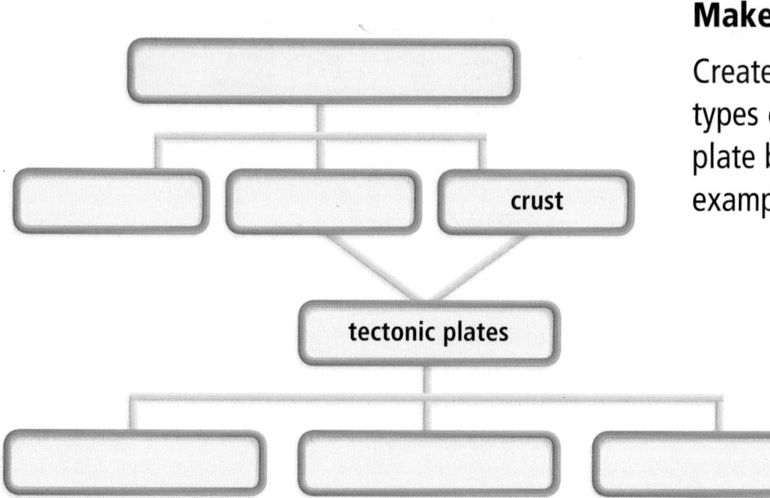

Critical Thinking

17. **Apply** The Himalaya Mountains lie on the northern border of India, which is also a plate boundary. Use plate tectonic theory to explain why Mt. Everest is increasing in height. What types of mountains are the Himalayas?

18. **Synthesize** As Alfred Wegener hypothesized, Pangaea was a supercontinent that ran north to south across the equator. North America was positioned over the equator. How might the climate of the United States have been different from today? What was the climate like in Antarctica?

19. **Apply** Why do tall mountains form at converging and diverging boundaries, but not typically at sliding boundaries?

20. **Synthesizing** During a strong earthquake, is the most damage done at the epicenter? Explain.

Performance Assessment

Make Mountains

Create a poster diagramming the three different types of mountains. Indicate the type of plate boundary, the type of mountain, and an example of where they occur.

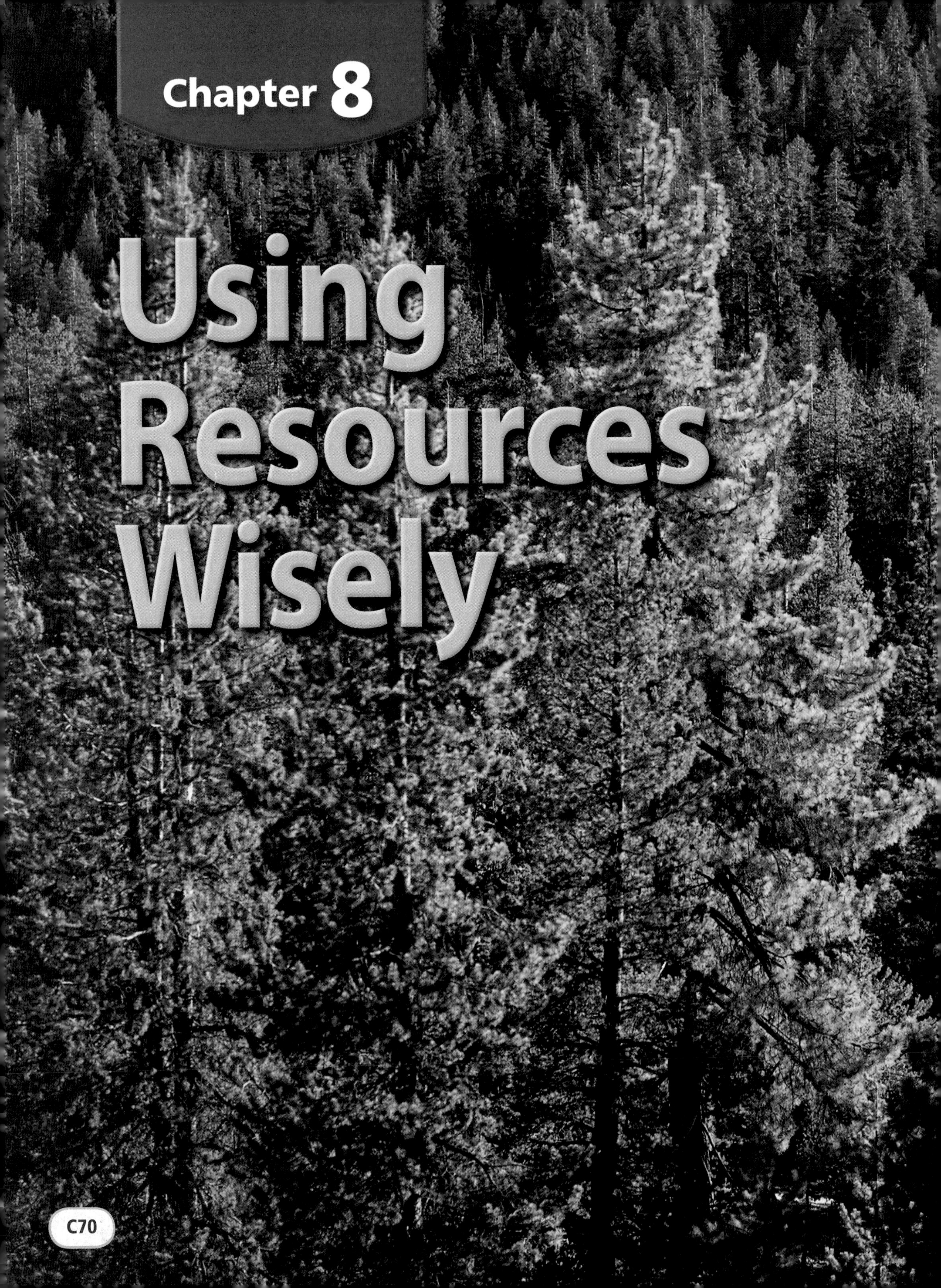

Chapter 8

Using Resources Wisely

Lesson Preview

LESSON 1

Cars, planes, and trucks—where do people get the energy to power vehicles?

Read about it in Lesson 1.

LESSON 2

Every day, wind and rain carry away soil. What problems can soil loss cause?

Read about it in Lesson 2.

LESSON 3

Reduce, reuse, recycle—how can you conserve Earth's valuable resources?

Read about it in Lesson 3.

Lesson 1

How Do People Use Resources?

Why It Matters...

You depend on natural resources for almost every activity of your life. Some resources, like the petroleum used to make gasoline, exist in limited supplies. When they are used up, they are gone forever. If people use resources wisely, everyone will have them for years to come.

PREPARE TO INVESTIGATE

Inquiry Skill

Use Models When you use models, you can see what happens in a real-world process.

Materials

- 3 plastic cups
- sand
- measuring cup
- teaspoon
- tablespoon
- goggles
- marking pen

Science and Math Toolbox

For step 3, review **Measuring Volume** on page H7.

Investigate

Just a Spoonful

Procedure

Safety: Wear goggles for this activity.

1. **Collaborate** Work with a partner. Label one cup "Natural Resource." Fill this cup with 100 ml of sand. Label a second cup "Resource Supply." Fill it with 100 ml of sand. In your *Science Notebook,* make a chart like the one shown.
2. **Use Models** One partner will be the "resource user" and will use a tablespoon to remove sand from the Natural Resource cup. The other will be the "resource supplier" and use a teaspoon to add sand to the cup. Spoon sand in and out of the cup at the same rate for 30 seconds.
3. **Measure** Measure and record the amount of sand remaining in the cup.
4. **Use Models** Refill the cup with 100 ml of sand. Repeat steps 2 and 3, but this time, only the resource user should spoon sand out of the cup. Do not add sand to the cup.

STEP 1

Use of Resources	Result
One student removing natural resource and one student supplying natural resource	
One student removing natural resource	

STEP 2

STEP 3

Conclusion

1. **Compare** What is the difference in the amount of sand in the Resource cup for the two trials? Explain the difference.
2. **Hypothesize** Based on the data, what do you think would happen in step 2 if both students were using the same size spoons?
3. **Use Models** What do the results show about natural resources?

Investigate More!

Design an Experiment
Repeat the activity, this time varying the speeds that you add or remove the sand. How does changing the rate affect the final amount of sand in the cup? Report your results in a chart, graph, or diagram.

Learn by Reading

Earth's Resources

VOCABULARY

READING SKILL

Problem and Solution
Use a diagram like the one below to compare possible solutions to the problem of limited natural resources.

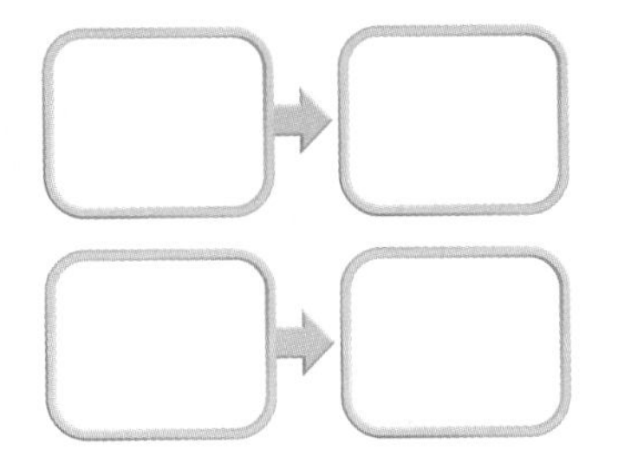

MAIN IDEA The Earth provides many resources that people need and use. Some resources are found only in limited quantities. Other resources are almost unlimited.

Natural Resources

The natural world provides everything that people need to stay alive, and many things that people find useful or helpful. These resources include air, water, minerals, and soil. They are called **natural resources.**

Humans have found many ways to take advantage of natural resources. We use them to build houses, grow crops, and raise livestock. We also use natural resources as a source of fuel and electrical energy. Natural resources that are used to produce energy are called energy resources.

Nuggets
Copper sometimes is found in pure nuggets like these. ▶

Mining
Copper comes from mines like the one here. Copper usually is found in combination with other elements. ▶

Nonrenewable Resources

Some natural resources are not easily replaced. These resources are called **nonrenewable resources.** Once a nonrenewable resource is used up, natural processes take millions of years to replace it.

Nonrenewable resources include oil, natural gas, and coal, which are examples of **fossil fuels.** They are called fossil fuels because they come from the remains of ancient plants and animals. Oil, which is also called petroleum, formed from the remains of plants and animals that once lived in the oceans.

How did plants and animals change into oil? After they died, their remains settled on the ocean floor. Over time, sediments built up on top of the remains, which were pressed under the building weight of the sediments. This pressure, along with heat from Earth's interior, changed the appearance and chemical makeup of the remains. Further pressure squeezed the remains into liquid. That liquid is oil.

Other nonrenewable resources include minerals and some rocks, such as ores of aluminum, iron, and copper. These materials are used for building materials and for making a wide range of products, from automobiles to jewelry.

Because nonrenewable resources cannot be replaced, it is important to use them wisely. If people are not careful, these resources will not be available for future generations.

PROBLEM AND SOLUTION **Why are fossil fuels examples of nonrenewable resources?**

Petroleum Formation

As marine plants and animals died, their remains were sometimes buried before they completely decomposed.

Over millions of years, heat and pressure turned this organic matter into oil.

The oil collected in fractured rocks or in spaces between sediment particles. Today, oil pumps remove the oil from these spaces.

Renewable Resources

Not all natural resources are nonrenewable. Resources that are easily replaced or that can be used over and over again are called **renewable resources.** Farm crops and animals are examples. So are oxygen and fresh water.

Trees are renewable resources because new ones can always be grown. People use trees to make paper products and for lumber. Wood from trees can also be burned as fuel. Many companies operate tree farms. For each tree that is cut down, a young tree is planted. Thus, the supply of trees is constantly renewed.

Trees are a valuable natural resource. By replacing cut-down trees, a tree farm can provide wood over and over again. ▼

Renewable resources that are used to produce energy are called alternative energy sources. They provide options to using fossil fuels.

Wind Windmills have been used for hundreds of years to move water and to grind grain. Today, wind farms use rows of wind turbines to power electric generators.

Like old-fashioned windmills, the turbines have blades that turn as the wind blows. The energy from the moving blades is converted into electricity.

Solar Energy from the Sun is called solar energy. Solar panels can collect sunlight and convert it to thermal energy. This energy can be used to heat homes. Other devices, called solar cells, convert the Sun's energy into electricity. Today, solar cells power calculators and electronic road signs. In the future, people may be driving solar-powered cars!

Water Power plants that use moving water to generate electricity are called hydroelectric plants. At these plants, water is held behind a dam and slowly released. The falling water turns turbines, similar to the way wind turns turbines. The energy is converted into electricity.

Today, people still use fossil fuels for much of their energy needs. Yet these fuels are becoming scarcer and more expensive. Developing alternative energy resources makes sense for the future!

PROBLEM AND SOLUTION How can people reduce their use of fossil fuels?

Wind

In windy places, wind turbines can generate electricity very efficiently.

Solar

Cars powered by solar energy must have a large surface area for solar cells. The solar cells collect the Sun's energy and convert it to electricity to power the car.

Water

Hydroelectric plants use the force of moving water to turn turbines. The energy from the spinning turbines is converted into electricity.

Most cars run on gasoline, a petroleum product. As petroleum reserves are used up, its cost is likely to rise even higher.

Conservation

The efficient use of resources is called **conservation.** Conserving nonrenewable resources is very important, because they cannot be replaced. By not wasting fossil fuels, you can save them for the future.

Another reason to conserve fossil fuels is to reduce pollution. Smoke from burning these fuels can mix with water in the air to form smog, which is not healthy to breathe.

Burning fuels adds a gas called carbon dioxide to the atmosphere. This action may be slowly warming Earth's temperature, an event called global warming. Scientists are studying this potential problem.

Other waste gases from fossil fuels mix with water in the air to form acid rain, another environmental problem. Acid rain can kill trees and fish, and damage buildings and statues.

What might be the most important natural resource to conserve? In many places, the answer is water. People need clean, fresh water for drinking, bathing, and growing crops. Although nature renews fresh water, the world's demand for water increases every year as the population grows.

You and your family can help to conserve Earth's important resources by following some simple, common-sense practices. Use public transportation, or form carpools. Turn off electric lights and appliances when not in use. Fix leaky faucets. What other ideas can you think of to practice conservation?

PROBLEM AND SOLUTION **What problem can conservation help to solve?**

Lesson Wrap-Up

Visual Summary

Natural resources are nonrenewable if they cannot be replaced in a person's lifetime.

Natural resources are renewable if they can be quickly and naturally replaced.

Alternative energy sources help people to conserve fossil fuels, a nonrenewable resource.

MATH **Create a Graph** Suppose a gasoline-powered car can travel 40 km (25 mi) on a gallon of gasoline. A car that uses a combination of gasoline and electricity can travel 96 km (60 mi) on a gallon of gasoline. Make a bar graph to show how far each car can travel on 25 gallons of gas.

TECHNOLOGY **Draw a Diagram** Research new technology that uses an alternative energy resource. Draw a diagram or illustration of the technology and present your display to the class.

Review

1. **MAIN IDEA** Why is solar energy called a renewable resource?

2. **VOCABULARY** Write a short paragraph using the terms *natural resource* and *energy resource.*

3. **READING SKILL: Problem and Solution** Which alternative energy resource do you think is most likely to replace fossil fuels in the future?

4. **CRITICAL THINKING: Evaluate** Where are the best places to build wind farms? Explain your reasoning.

5. **INQUIRY SKILL: Use Models** A student constructs a model of a natural resource using a can with a small hole in the bottom. With the hole plugged, the can is filled with sand. When the plug is removed, the sand drains out. What kind of resource does this model illustrate?

TEST PREP

Which of the following is a renewable resource?

A. oil

B. natural gas

C. lumber

D. aluminum

Technology
Visit **www.eduplace.com/scp/** to find out more about natural resources.

Hybrid Cars

In many ways, hybrid cars look and operate much like other modern cars. The difference is inside. Hybrids are powered by a combination of gasoline and electricity!

As you read about hybrid cars, compare them to conventional cars that run on gasoline only. What advantages do you think hybrid cars provide?

Instruments

This gauge shows the volume of gas in the tank and the charge of the battery. ▼

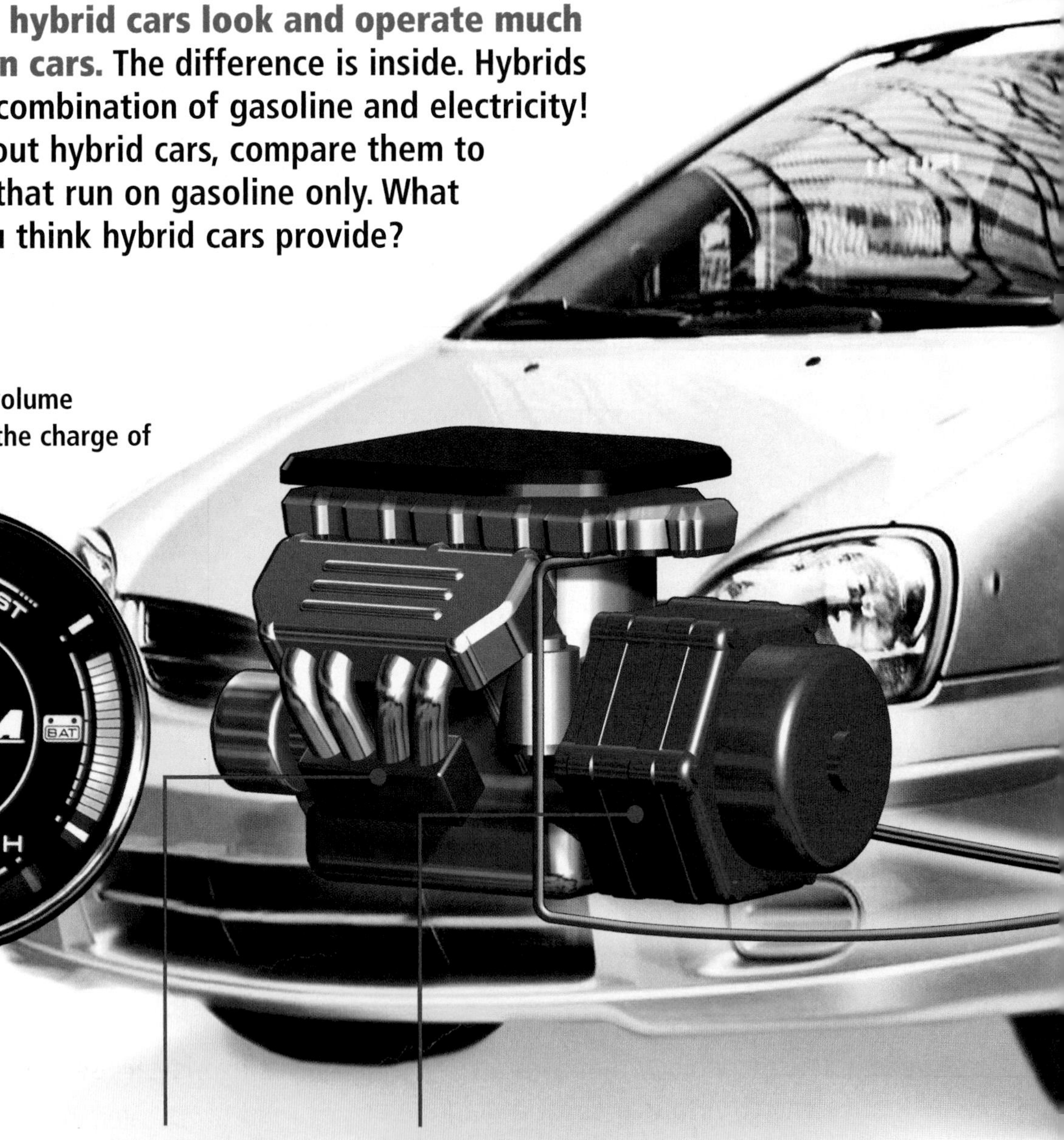

Gasoline Engine

The engine is smaller and more fuel-efficient than the engines of most cars. It pollutes less, too.

Electric Motor

The motor draws energy from the batteries to accelerate the car. Yet it also can act as a generator, using the energy of the moving car to recharge the batteries.

How Hybrid Cars Work

Battery
Discharge Recharge

When the car travels uphill, the battery discharges to add extra power to the car's engine.

Battery
Discharge Recharge

On level surfaces, the car uses one or both power sources, depending on its speed.

Battery
Discharge Recharge

When the car travels downhill, the motor converts to an electric generator. It recharges the battery.

Gas Tank

One popular brand of hybrid car can travel more than 1,000 km (630 mi) on a single tank of gas.

Batteries

In a completely electric-powered car, batteries take up a lot of the car's volume. Because a hybrid car needs less battery power, its batteries take up less space.

Sharing Ideas

1. **READING CHECK** How do batteries help a hybrid car use less gasoline?
2. **WRITE ABOUT IT** Describe the advantages of hybrid cars.
3. **TALK ABOUT IT** How do hybrid cars compare to cars that run on gasoline only?

Lesson 2

How Do People Use Soil?

Why It Matters...

Plants need mature, nutrient-rich soil in order to grow. Plants in turn protect and enrich soil. By studying how plants and soil interact, you can help protect both.

PREPARE TO INVESTIGATE

Inquiry Skill

Observe When you observe, you use what you can see or measure to help you draw a conclusion.

Materials

- 2 plastic bowls
- measuring cup
- moist soil
- plastic wrap
- goggles

Science and Math Toolbox

For steps 2 to 4, review **Making a Chart to Organize Data** on page H11.

Investigate

A Mighty Wind!

Procedure

Safety: Wear goggles for this activity.

1. **Collaborate** Work with a partner. Place 250 mL (1 cup) of moist soil in each of the two plastic bowls. Label the soil samples A and B. In your *Science Notebook*, create a chart like the one shown.

2. **Observe** Test the soil samples to determine their characteristics. For example, feel the consistency, dampness, and texture of the soil. Blow on it to see what effect wind might have on it. Record your observations.

3. **Experiment** Securely cover soil sample A with plastic wrap. Make sure there are no holes or gaps in the wrap. Leave soil sample B open. Place the two bins in a warm, sunny window and leave them overnight.

4. **Observe** Remove the plastic wrap from sample A. Repeat step 2 with both samples and record your observations.

STEP 1

Soil Quality	Sample A	Sample B
Day 1		
Day 2		

STEP 2

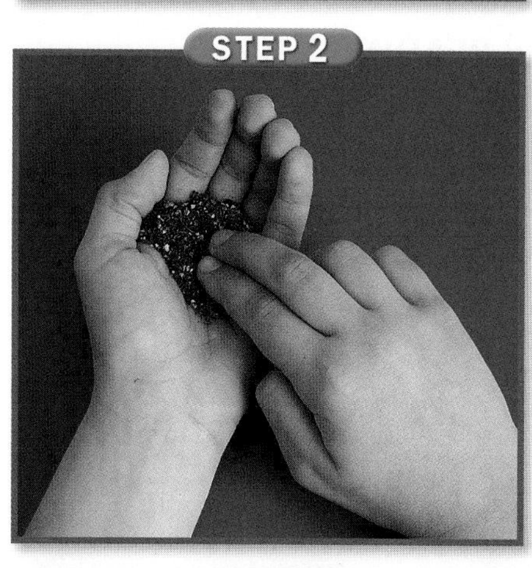

STEP 3

Conclusion

1. **Compare** Compare your data about the two soil samples. What similarities and differences do you notice? How do you explain them?

2. **Infer** How do you think your observations might explain soil conditions in nature?

3. **Hypothesize** Do you think that growing plants affect the way that soil holds water? How could you test your hypothesis?

Investigate More!

Design an Experiment
Will soil, sand, and gravel dry out at different rates? Design an experiment to find out. Conduct the experiment with your teacher's approval.

Learn by Reading

Uses of Soil

VOCABULARY

READING SKILL

Draw Conclusions Use a chart to record your conclusions about what conditions produce the best soil.

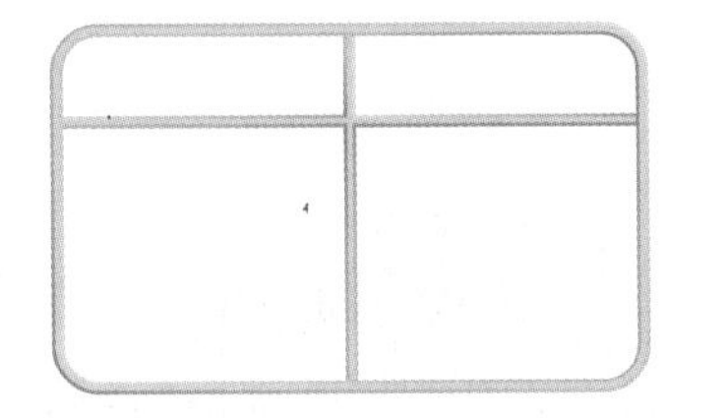

MAIN IDEA **Soil supports the growth of crops and other plants. Soil must be protected because mature, nutrient-rich soil takes a long time to form.**

What is Soil?

Soil is a natural resource that is made up of minerals and small rocks, water, gases, and organic matter. The minerals and small rocks are weathered bedrock. The organic matter, called humus, is decayed plant and animal material.

Not all soils are alike. Different geographic areas have different types of soil. For example, the soil in a desert will be very different from soil in a forest.

The type of soil a place has depends on several factors. These factors include climate and the types of rocks and organic matter present in the area. The size of the particles in soil may describe the soil's texture. Study the types of soil shown below. How do you think the quality of soil affects the plants that grow in it?

Sandy Soil
In sandy soil, particles are medium-sized and very hard. ▲

Clay soil
Clay soil is made up of very small, tightly-packed mineral particles. ▲

Rocky soil
Rocky soil, or gravel, includes relatively large fragments of rock. ▲

How Soil Is Formed

Soil forms in a process that takes thousands of years. This process begins with weathering. As you learned in Chapter 6, weathering is the breaking down of rock into smaller pieces of rocks and minerals.

If you were to dig a hole deep enough, you would hit bedrock. Bedrock is unweathered rock beneath the soil and other loose material on Earth's surface.

As the upper part of the bedrock weathers, it breaks into smaller pieces. These pieces eventually become part of the mixture called soil. Soil that forms from the bedrock beneath is called **residual soil.**

Sometimes, the soil in an area has minerals that are different from those in the bedrock below. This soil, called **transported soil,** has been carried from some other location by wind and water.

As soil forms, plants begin to grow. After plants and animals die, their remains decay. Rain carries the decayed organic material, or humus, from the surface into the developing soil. Humus adds nutrients to soil.

Plant roots, insects, worms, and other organisms also help in the development of nutrient-rich soil. Roots grow into the soil, and insects and worms burrow in it. They create spaces between the soil particles. These spaces allow air to circulate and more humus to collect.

DRAW CONCLUSIONS **How does the bedrock affect the type of soil in an area?**

Earthworms, bacteria, and fungi break down dead plant and animal material. The remains add nutrients to the soil.

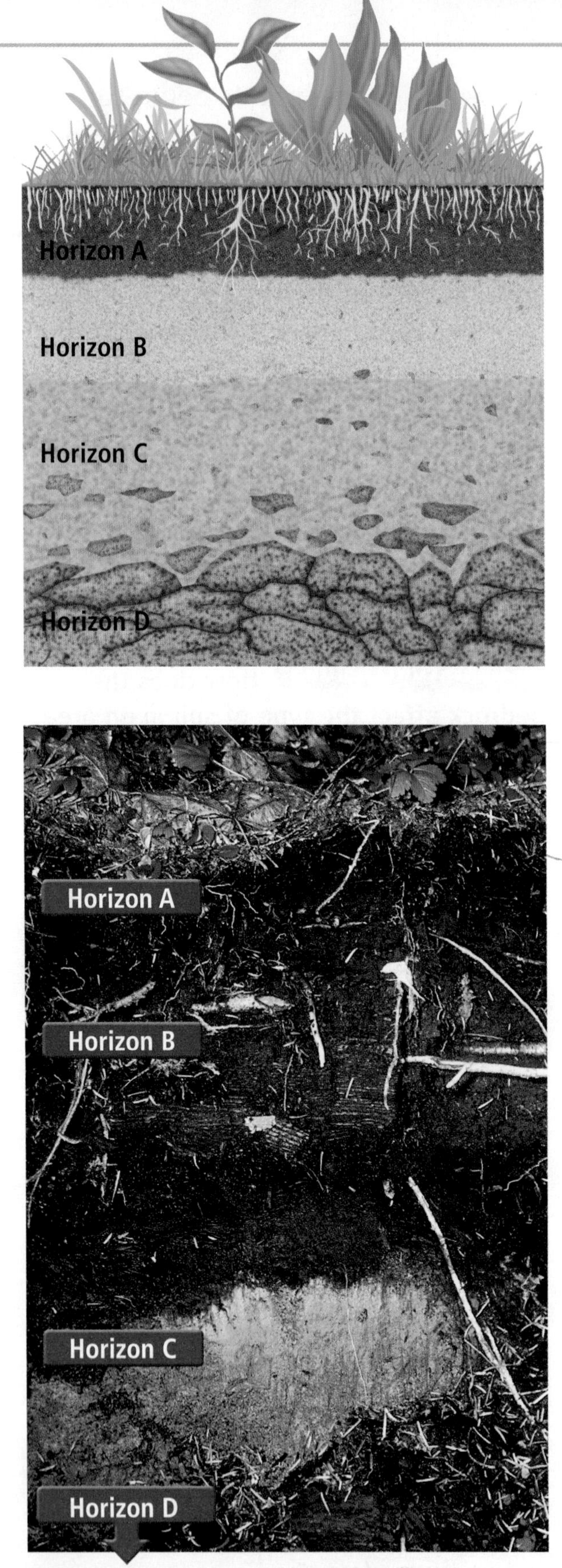

The action of water, plants, and animals created the mature soil profile shown here. ▲

Profile of Mature Soil

Over time, as soil develops, definite layers can be observed. These layers are called soil horizons. A mature soil has four horizons. Young or immature soil has fewer horizons.

All of the soil horizons together are called a **soil profile.** In a mature soil profile, from the top down, the horizons are called topsoil, subsoil, parent material, and bedrock. The layers are also given letter names, as shown in the diagram.

Horizon A is the **topsoil.** Topsoil contains humus, minerals and rock fragments, as well as insects and earthworms. This part of the soil has the most nutrients and is important for growing plants. Most plant seeds germinate, or sprout, in topsoil.

Horizon B is the **subsoil.** Subsoil usually contains very little humus. However, water washes down some nutrients and organic matter from the topsoil. Some plant roots may reach down into the subsoil, and some earthworms and other organisms may be found here.

The next layer, horizon C, is made up of chunks of partly weathered bedrock. This rock is sometimes called the parent material, because the soil comes from it.

Below the parent material is the bedrock, or horizon D. This thick layer of rock is the foundation for the soil.

DRAW CONCLUSIONS **What can you learn from studying a soil profile?**

Crop Rotation Schedule

	Field 1	Field 3	Field 5
Year 1	Wheat	Wheat	Wheat
Year 2	Canola	Canola	Corn
Year 3	Barley	Corn	Canola
Year 4	Flax	Sunflower	Flax
Year 5	Soybean	Barley	Alfalfa

▲ These crops are different from those that were grown in the same fields a season ago.

◀ This table shows several recommended crop rotation schedules for northeast North Dakota.

Protecting Topsoil

As you have learned, topsoil is the layer of soil that has the most nutrients. Plants use these nutrients in a way that is comparable to how your body uses vitamins. While the nutrients are not food for plants, they are necessary for healthy growth.

The nutrients are passed on to animals that eat the plants, and to animals that eat the plant-eaters. Organic material from these plants and animals then returns the nutrients to the soil. This cycle is important to all living things.

Farmers must meet the challenge of maintaining nutrients in the soil. Growing crops take nutrients out of the soil. When the crops are harvested, the nutrients are removed with them.

How do farmers solve this problem? One solution is to add fertilizer to the soil to replace the nutrients. This solution is not perfect, however, because some of the fertilizer washes away when it rains.

Another way of returning nutrients to the soil is through crop rotation. Crop rotation is the planting of different crops during different growing seasons. Each type of plant uses different sets of nutrients.

If the same crop is grown in the same field for many years, the same nutrients are removed from the soil. With crop rotation, the soil is naturally replenished.

DRAW CONCLUSIONS **According to the chart, if corn is grown in a field in Year 3, what crop should be planted in Year 4?**

Conserving Topsoil

Farmers have found ways to prevent soil from losing nutrients. However, topsoil also needs to be protected from wind, water, and other agents of erosion.

What can be the result of excessive soil erosion? People learned the hard answer in the 1930s. Up until then, many farmers in the Great Plains practiced poor soil management. As a result, crops sometimes were poor and the topsoil was left bare. Conditions worsened during a long drought, which dried the topsoil. Winds simply picked up the topsoil and carried it away.

The region where this happened became known as the Dust Bowl. Huge dust storms swept across the area, and winds carried soil far from the farmlands. Without topsoil, farmers were unable to grow crops for many years. Without crops, a food shortage set in.

Experts estimate that about 850 million tons of topsoil were lost in the dust storms of 1935. Today, in part because of better soil conservation, that land is fertile again. ▼

Today, farmers follow much smarter soil conservation plans. One way farmers prevent wind erosion of the topsoil is by creating windbreaks, or shelterbelts. A windbreak is a line of trees planted along the edge of a field. The trees help block the wind and prevent or reduce soil erosion.

Water is another factor in soil erosion. When water moves down the slopes of a plowed field, it picks up soil and carries it away. To reduce this type of erosion, farmers practice contour plowing. They follow the contours of their fields as they plow. These winding furrows slow water down as gravity moves it down the slope.

Another approach to preventing soil erosion is to plant cover crops, such as clover or alfalfa. The roots of these plants hold soil in place and prevent it from being carried away.

DRAW CONCLUSIONS **How do plants help protect soil?**

Lesson Wrap-Up

Visual Summary

Soil is made up of weathered rock material, gases, water, and humus. Decaying plants and animals add nutrients to the soil.

Topsoil is important because it provides most of the nutrients for growing plants.

Conservation practices help farmers prevent the loss of topsoil through erosion. "Dust Bowls" can be prevented.

MATH **Estimate Using Fractions** A farmer practices crop rotation to conserve soil nutrients. She grows wheat one year in every five. About what fraction of her total crop output is wheat?

WRITING **Narrative** Find out more about the Dust Bowl of the 1930s. Write a short story describing what it must have been like to be a farmer in the Great Plains during the 1930s.

Review

1. **MAIN IDEA** What layers make up a mature soil profile?
2. **VOCABULARY** In your own words, define the term *soil profile.*
3. **READING SKILL: Draw Conclusions** You notice that the steep sides of a highway road cut are covered in tightly woven netting. What might be the reason for this practice?
4. **CRITICAL THINKING: Analyze** Why do farmers need to understand the nutrients required by the crops that they plant?
5. **INQUIRY SKILL: Observe** You dig up part of your yard in hopes of planting a garden. You see that the uppermost layer of soil is thin, and you find a lot of rocks near the surface. What does this tell you about how your garden will grow?

TEST PREP

The layer of mature soil that contains only a few nutrients is the

A. bedrock.

B. parent material.

C. subsoil.

D. topsoil.

Technology

Visit **www.eduplace.com/scp/** to find out more about soil.

Lesson 3

How Can People Use Resources Wisely?

Why It Matters...

Why should you recycle old bottles and cans? One reason is to conserve Earth's resources. Recycling plastics, metals, and other materials means they can be used to make new products.

PREPARE TO INVESTIGATE

Inquiry Skill

Collaborate When you collaborate, you work with other people to find solutions by considering the suggestions, findings, and ideas of others.

Science and Math Toolbox

For steps 2 to 4, review **Making a Chart to Organize Data** on page H11.

Investigate

Recycling!

Procedure

1. **Collaborate** As a class, identify all the materials that your family, your school, and your community recycle.

2. **Record Data** In your *Science Notebook,* list the materials that the class identified. Create a chart like the one shown.

3. **Predict** Review your list and choose two types of recyclable materials that your household uses. Predict how many of these recyclable items your household uses in a week. Then predict how many of the goods will be recycled. Record your predictions.

4. **Observe** For one week, monitor your household's use of the selected recyclable goods. Record how many items are recycled and how many are thrown in the trash.

STEP 2

	Predicted data		Observed data	
	Used	Recycled	Used	Recycled
Glass bottles				
Newspaper				
Plastic				
Aluminum cans				

STEP 4

Conclusion

1. **Analyze Data** Use your data to calculate the total amount of your chosen recyclable goods used in your household that week. Then, calculate the percentage of those materials that were set aside to be recycled. Did your household recycle more or less than it threw in the trash?

2. **Collaborate** Work in a small group to develop a plan that would encourage people in your community to recycle more.

Investigate More!

Solve a Problem
From your data or other observations, choose a resource that you think is wasted in your community. How could this resource be used wisely? Present your ideas in a letter, poster, or skit.

Learn by Reading

Conservation

▶ **VOCABULARY**

recycling p. C92

▶ **READING SKILL**

Problem and Solution
Use a chart to compare the pros and cons of one of the conservation solutions discussed in this lesson.

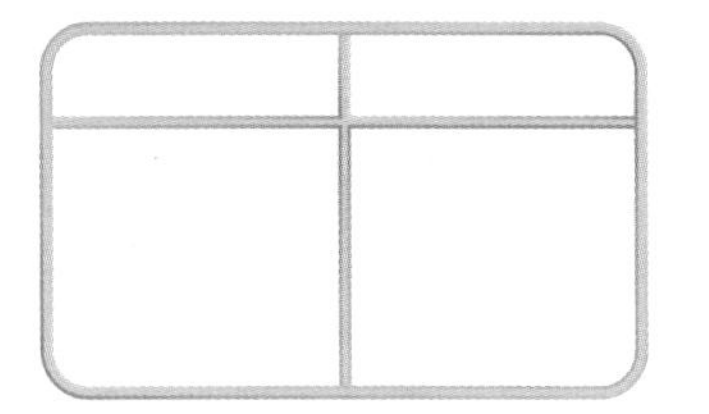

MAIN IDEA By reducing, reusing, and recycling, people can help ensure that important resources used to make everyday items will be available in the future.

Using Resources Wisely

Think about some of the things you used today—a plastic water bottle, an aluminum can, a paper towel. These are very useful items, and all come from natural resources. Plastic is a petroleum-based product. Aluminum comes from a mineral ore that is mined. Paper is made from trees.

When you finished using these items, what did you do with them? Did you throw them away in the trash? If so, the resources used to make these items are lost. But it doesn't have to be that way.

Recycling means recovering a resource from one item and using that resource to make another item. Recycling saves energy and conserves resources.

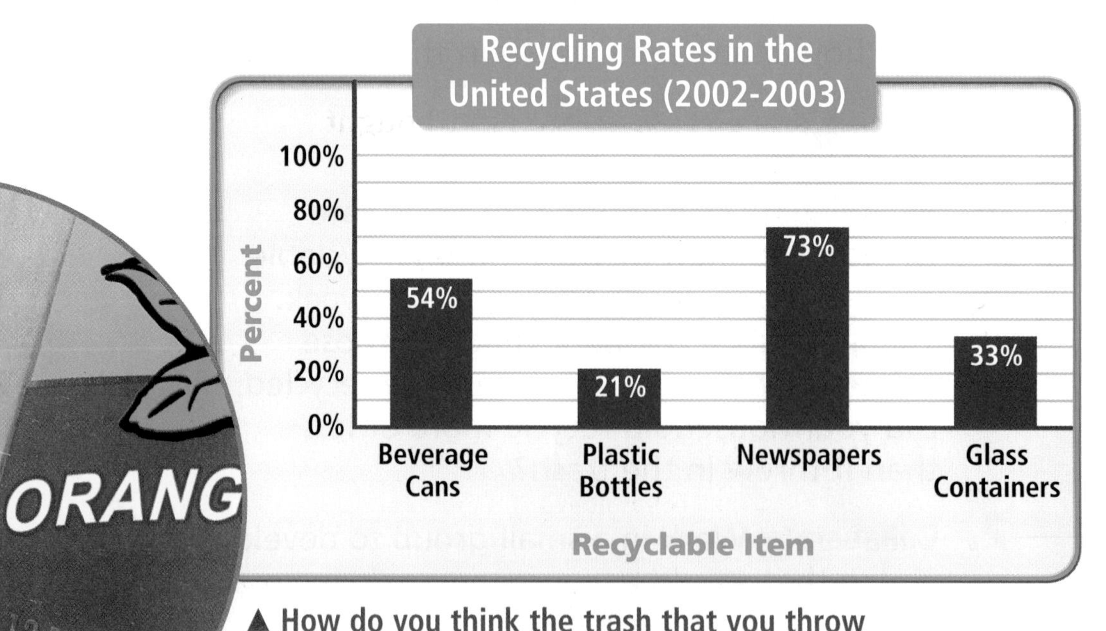

▲ How do you think the trash that you throw out compares to the data shown here?

◀ **Recycle**
The triple-arrow symbol means that this can should be recycled.

The Three Rs of Conservation

There are three main ways to conserve resources: reduce, reuse, and recycle. People refer to these as the three Rs of conservation. You have already learned how recycling helps conserve resources.

Reducing simply means using less material. For example, when you use one paper towel to wipe up a spill instead of using two, you reduce your use of paper. If you choose not to use a straw in your drink, you reduce the amount of plastic you use. Every time you walk or ride a bike instead of riding in a car, you reduce the amount of fossil fuels that you use.

Reusing is another way to conserve resources. Reusing can be as simple as using a glass cup again and again instead of throwing away a plastic cup after a single use.

Reusing also means putting things to new uses. For example, you could wash an empty plastic pickle jar and keep it on your desk as a pencil holder. This keeps the jar from ending up in the garbage. It also saves the material that would have been used to make a pencil holder that you otherwise might have bought at a store.

In general, reducing and reusing are more effective than recycling. Both save more resources and energy than recycling does. But recycling resources is still much better than wasting them.

PROBLEM AND SOLUTION **How does recycling help to conserve natural resources?**

▲ Reduce
Insulation helps reduce the amount of energy used in buildings. This fiberglass insulation helps keep a house cool in the summer and warm in the winter.

Reuse
These containers and cloth diapers can be used over and over again. What other reusable items can you name? ▶

Landfills

Have you ever wondered what happens to the trash that you throw away? You may know that a truck picks it up, but where does the truck take it?

Most trash ends up in a landfill. A landfill is a place where trash is deposited and then covered with plastic or clay. The plastic or clay seals the trash in the landfill and keeps the wastes contained.

Landfills are carefully designed to keep waste in and water and air out. This design has both benefits and drawbacks. The sealing of landfills keeps materials in the waste from polluting the environment. Harmful chemicals are stopped from seeping into the groundwater. Yet the lack of air and water slows the rate that the wastes decompose, or break down.

Most organic matter, such as paper or leather, will decompose fairly quickly when exposed to air and water. However, when sealed in a landfill, they might take several years to break down. Other wastes can take hundreds of years to decompose. Trash you throw out today may remain in landfills for a very long time.

Each landfill is designed to take up a certain amount of space. Once it is filled, it must be closed. Some communities have no more space to create new landfills. They must ship their trash to other areas for disposal.

When we reduce, reuse, and recycle items that would otherwise be thrown out as trash, we decrease the amount of material that is sent to landfills. Not only are resources conserved, but space in landfills is also conserved.

PROBLEM AND SOLUTION **Why must landfills be carefully designed?**

Landfills take up valuable land resources. Practicing the three Rs reduces the trash that goes to the landfill.

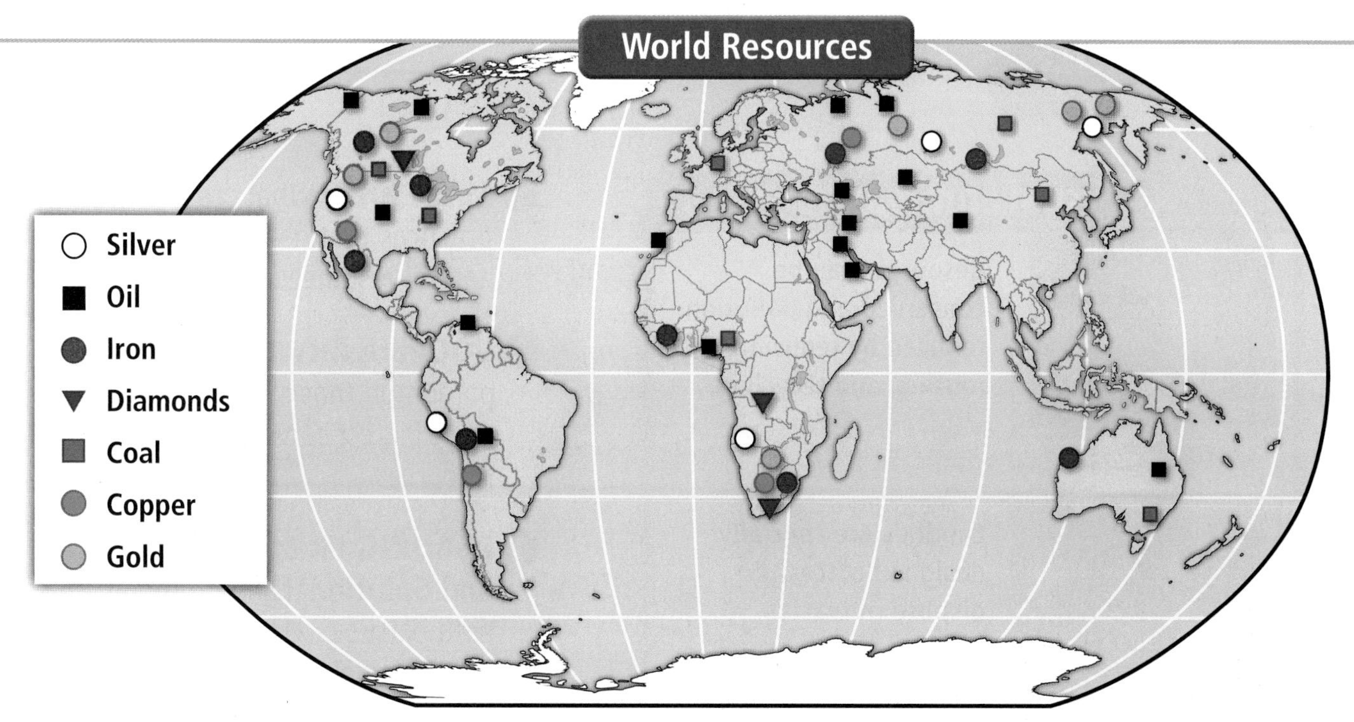

This map shows where natural resources are found. When resources are not located near where they are used, other resources must be used to transport them. ▲

Where the Resources Are

The map on this page shows places around the world that have large deposits of different natural resources. You can see that many resources are found only in certain parts of the world.

In the past, people often settled in areas where important resources were found. The natural resources available in an area shaped the lives and businesses of communities in the region. While this is still true to some extent, modern transportation and technology make it much easier for people to use and rely on resources from all over the world.

Today, people commonly transport resources. A resource such as silver may be taken from the place it is mined and shipped to another place to be processed. Pure silver is then shipped all over the world to jewelers and other manufacturers.

Oil is one resource that is used everywhere, but found in large supplies in only a few places. Every day, ships carry millions of gallons of oil across the oceans.

These ships sometimes have accidents, and their cargoes spill into the water. Oil spills can be deadly to fish, whales, seals, and other marine life. Eventually, the oil can wash up on land and damage ecosystems along the shore.

Transporting resources around the world brings many benefits. However, it can also be costly and harm the environment. When people conserve natural resources through the three Rs of conservation, fewer resources need to be shipped around the world.

PROBLEM AND SOLUTION **What is one solution to the problems caused by transporting oil?**

Lesson Wrap-Up

Visual Summary

Resources can be conserved and pollution reduced by reducing, reusing, and recycling.

Landfills are specially designed places to dispose of wastes.

Natural resources are transported regularly from regions where they are found to other regions where they are used.

MATH **Make a Graph** Use newspapers, almanacs, and the Internet to find out the average amount of trash produced by a nearby city each year for the last five years. Make a line graph showing the data. Analyze the trends you find.

TECHNOLOGY **Write a Report** Research developments in the design and location of landfills. Write a report explaining what you learned.

Review

1. **MAIN IDEA** What are three practices that help conserve natural resources?
2. **VOCABULARY** Write a short paragraph that explains how recycling conserves natural resources.
3. **READING SKILL: Problem and Solution** Landfills are lined with plastic or clay. What problem does this help to solve?
4. **CRITICAL THINKING: Apply** Cobalt is a metal used in making powerful magnets. The United States imports all its cobalt from other countries. If large cobalt deposits were found in the Rocky Mountains, how might that affect the United States and other countries?
5. **INQUIRY SKILL: Collaborate** Work with a partner to list three ways of reducing the use of natural resources at your school.

TEST PREP

Which of the following is NOT a method of conserving resources?

A. replace

B. recycle

C. reuse

D. reduce

Technology

Visit **www.eduplace.com/scp/** to find out more about how resources can be used wisely.

Cartographer

Cartographers are map makers. They map many types of surface features, from the highest mountain to the ocean floor. Maps may present natural features, such as elevation and climate, or human-made ones, such as cities, roads, and crops.

Cartographers rely on physical surveys, as well as images from airplanes and satellites. They often use computers, too.

What It Takes!

- A degree in geography, geology, or art
- Drawing and computer skills

Farmer

Is farming the most important job in the world? Nearly all of the world's food comes from crops and livestock raised by farmers and ranchers. So do many other products, such as cotton, leather, and wool.

Farmers must do many tasks: operate and care for farm machinery, monitor weather conditions, prevent crop and animal diseases, care for the soil, and manage a business.

What It Takes!

- Courses in agriculture and business
- Energy for strenuous work outdoors

Extreme Science

TIRED!

What a waste! It took millions of gallons of fossil fuel and many other nonrenewable resources to make the tires in this picture. Every year hundreds of millions of tires are thrown away. Experts estimate there are at least 1 *billion* scrap tires in the United States!

Because tires take up to 80 years to decompose, they aren't going away soon. Fortunately, recycling tires has become big business. Each year, more and more old tires are processed to produce fuel. Tires are also ground up and used to create safe, sturdy surfaces for roads, sidewalks, and playgrounds.

Run a rope through the billion tires in U.S. landfills today. You'll have a tire necklace long enough to circle the earth 5 times!

Tire Doctor

Dr. Jagdish Dhawan, shown here, worked with fellow chemistry professor Richard Legendre to develop a new process that recycles scrap tires into high-grade oil without any waste.

Vocabulary

Complete each sentence with a term from the list.

1. Sending aluminum cans to a plant to be made into other aluminum products is an example of ____.
2. A(n) ____ is anything found in nature that is necessary or useful to humans.
3. Coal is called a(n) ____ because it formed from the remains of ancient living things.
4. The layers that make up a mature soil represent the ____.
5. Humus is most commonly found in ____.
6. The layer of soil with little or no organic matter is called ____.
7. ____ is soil that is located where it formed.
8. A(n) ____ may only be used once because it cannot be replaced.
9. Soil that has been carried by wind or water from where it formed is called ____.
10. A(n) ____ may be used repeatedly, because it can be replaced.

conservation C80
fossil fuel C77
natural resource C76
nonrenewable resource C77
recycling C94
renewable resource C78
residual soil C87
soil C86
soil profile C88
subsoil C88
topsoil C88
transported soil C87

Test Prep

Write the letter of the best answer choice.

11. The practice of using all resources wisely is called ____.

    A. conservation
    B. using renewable resources
    C. using nonrenewable resources
    D. composting

12. Which is NOT a common part of soil?

    A. humus
    B. water
    C. minerals
    D. fossil fuels

13. What is one example of capturing a renewable energy source?

    A. mining for coal
    B. mining for oil
    C. installing wind turbines
    D. drinking a glass of water

14. Using china dishes instead of paper plates is an example of ____ paper use.

    A. reducing
    B. reusing
    C. recycling
    D. unwise

Inquiry Skills

15. Observe How could you use the appearance of a creek after a rainstorm to determine if soil erosion is taking place?

16. Collaborate How might people work together to reduce the amount of trash that is sent to a landfill? Discuss positive steps that families, businesses, and communities can take.

Map the Concept

This chart shows two categories. Classify each of these natural resources.

coal
oil
trees
solar energy
natural gas
wind energy
moving water

Renewable Resource	Nonrenewable Resource

Critical Thinking

17. Evaluate How would you respond to people who say it is not necessary to conserve fossil fuels, because the supply of fossil fuels will not run out during their lifetime?

18. Apply Name three different types of resources that people mine from Earth. Describe uses for these resources.

19. Apply If you were interviewing a company to pick up your materials for recycling, what are three questions you would ask?

20. Analyze What natural resources are especially common in your state? How do people collect or use them? Research your state's resources at the library or on the Internet.

Performance Assessment

Plowing a Field

Suppose a farmer wanted to check on the quality of his soil from one year to the next. Make a list of steps he could take to gather this information. Explain how each action would help him detect any changes in soil quality.

UNIT C Review and Test Prep

Write the letter of the best answer choice.

1. Rosa keeps her pens and pencils in an old tennis ball can. Which conservation strategy is this?

A. recycle
B. reduce
C. resource
D. reuse

2. Which surface feature do living organisms build up?

A. coral reef
B. river delta
C. shield cone
D. terminal moraine

3. The diagram shows which type of plate boundary?

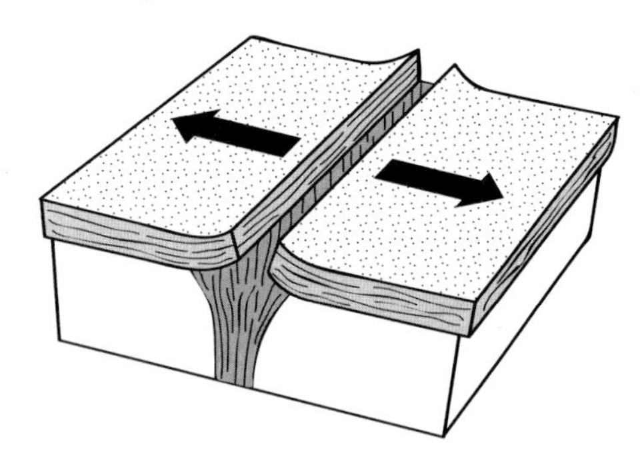

A. converging
B. diverging
C. sliding
D. subducting

4. Soil that forms from the bedrock below it is called ________ .

A. humus.
B. rocky soil.
C. residual soil.
D. transported soil.

5. Which is a nonrenewable energy source?

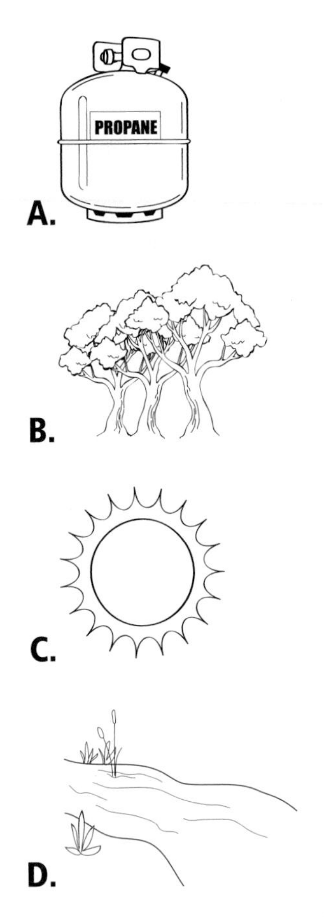

6. Which of the following provide evidence to support the theory of continental drift?

A. atolls
B. caves
C. deltas
D. fossils

7. Which of the following is NOT a feature of the deep ocean floor?

   A. guyot

   B. seamount

   C. abyssal plain

   D. continental margin

8. Which represents a destructive force on Earth's surface?

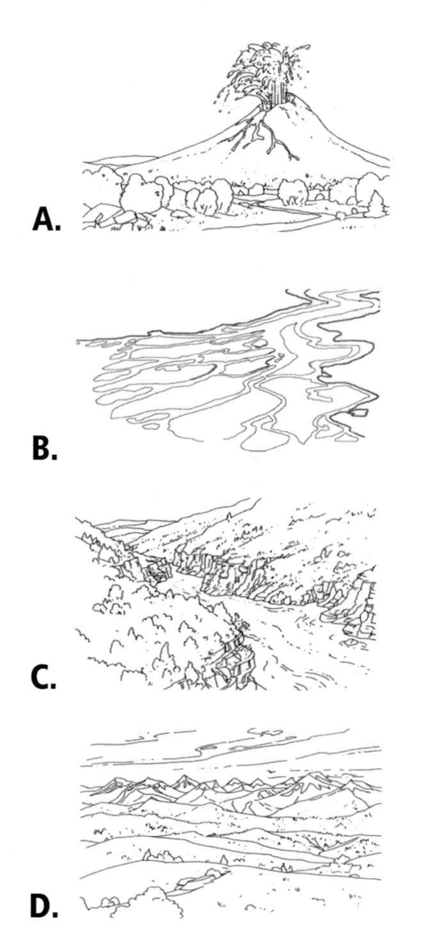

Answer the following in complete sentences.

9. Hybrid cars run on gasoline some of the time and on electric power the rest of the time. What conservation strategy applies to hybrid cars? Explain your answer.

10. Earthquakes generate three kinds of waves: S waves, P waves, and L waves. Which wave type causes the MOST damage? Explain your answer.

On January 17, 1994, a strong earthquake struck southern California. The epicenter was near the community of Northridge, and the magnitude was 6.7 on the Richter scale. The map shows how strongly the shaking was felt in different communities.

Richter Scale

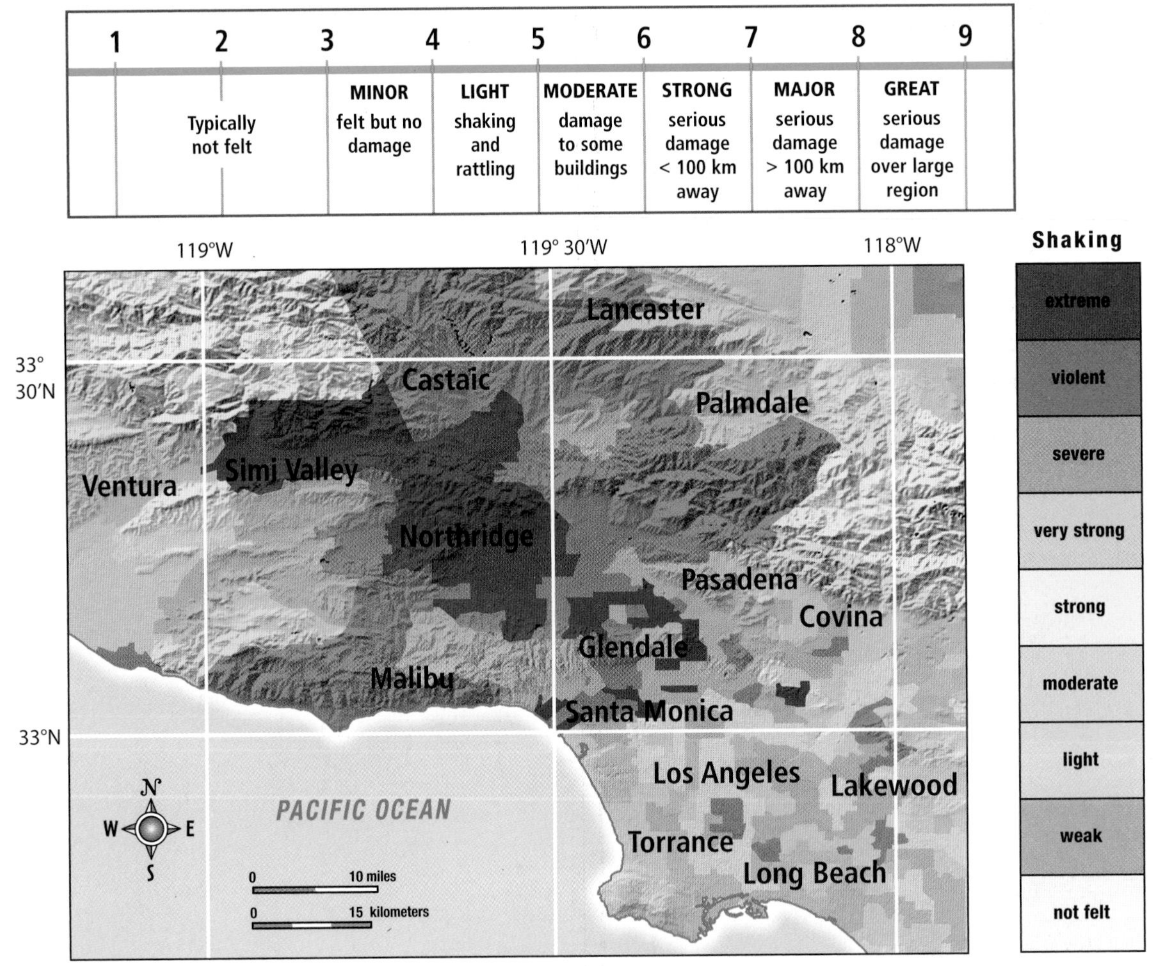

Earthquakes strike when rocks suddenly break deep below Earth's surface. In a severe earthquake, the shock waves can topple buildings and collapse bridges. Earthquakes are common along the edge of the Pacific Ocean, where tectonic plates are slowly sliding against one another.

See an earthquake in action. Go to **www.eduplace.com/scp/** to view a Flash™ movie and to learn more about earthquakes.

Science and Math Toolbox

Using a Microscope

A microscope makes it possible to see very small things by magnifying them. Some microscopes have a set of lenses that magnify objects by different amounts.

Examine Some Salt Grains

Handle a microscope carefully; it can break easily. Carry it firmly with both hands and avoid touching the lenses.

1. Turn the mirror toward a source of light. **NEVER** use the Sun as a light source.

2. Place a few grains of salt on the slide. Put the slide on the stage of the microscope.

3. Bring the salt grains into focus. Turn the adjustment knob on the back of the microscope as you look through the eyepiece.

4. Raise the eyepiece tube to increase the magnification; lower it to decrease magnification.

Making a Bar Graph

A bar graph helps you organize and compare data. For example, you might want to make a bar graph to compare weather data for different places.

Make a Bar Graph of Annual Snowfall

For more than 20 years, the cities listed in the table have been recording their yearly snowfall. The table shows the average number of centimeters of snow that the cities receive each year. Use the data in the table to make a bar graph showing the cities' average annual snowfall.

Snowfall

City	Snowfall (cm)
Atlanta, GA	5
Charleston, SC	1.5
Houston, TX	1
Jackson, MS	3
New Orleans, LA	0.5
Tucson, AZ	3

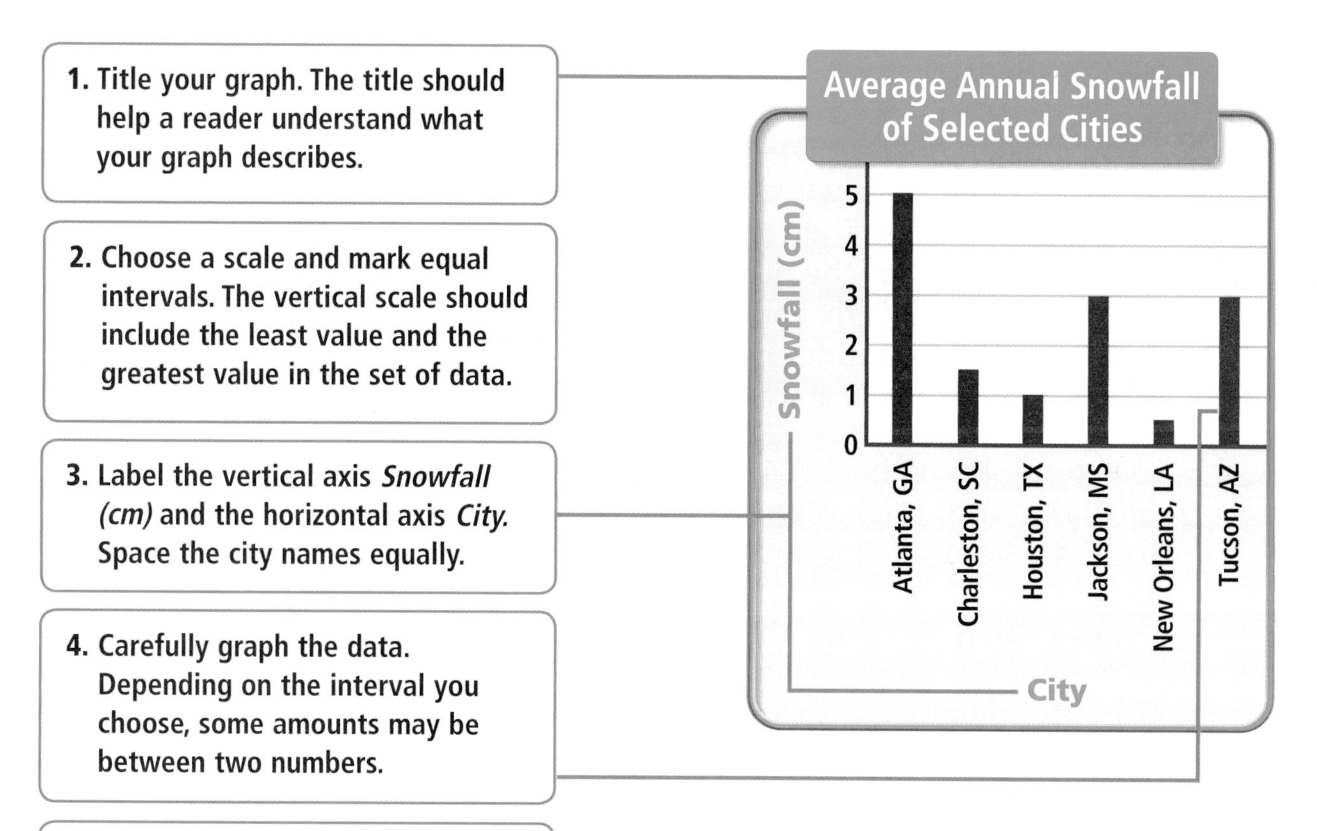

5. Check each step of your work.

Using a Calculator

After you've made measurements, a calculator can help you analyze your data. Some calculators have a memory key that allows you to save the result of one calculation while you do another.

Add and Divide to Find Percent

The table shows the amount of rain that was collected using a rain gauge in each month of one year. You can use a calculator to help you find the total yearly rainfall. Then you can find the percent of rain that fell during January.

Rainfall

Month	Rain (mm)
Jan.	214
Feb.	138
Mar.	98
Apr.	157
May	84
June	41
July	5
Aug.	23
Sept.	48
Oct.	75
Nov.	140
Dec.	108

1. Add the numbers. When you add a series of numbers, you need not press the equal sign until the last number is entered. Just press the plus sign after you enter each number (except the last).

2. If you make a mistake while you are entering numbers, press the clear entry (CE/C) key to erase your mistake. Then you can continue entering the rest of the numbers you are adding. If you can't fix your mistake, you can press the (CE/C) key once or twice until the screen shows 0. Then start over.

3. Your total should be 1,131. Now clear the calculator until the screen shows 0. Then divide the rainfall amount for January by the total yearly rainfall (1,131). Press the percent (%) key. Then press the equal sign key.

214 ÷ 1131 % =

The percent of yearly rainfall that fell in January is 18.921309, which rounds to 19%.

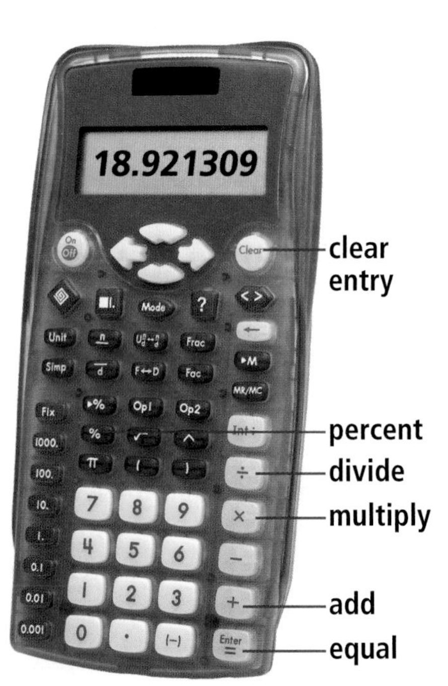

Finding an Average

An average is a way to describe a set of data using one number. For example, you could compare the surface temperature of several stars that are of the same type. You could find the average surface temperature of these stars.

Add and Divide to Find the Average

Suppose scientists found the surface temperature of eight blue-white stars to be those shown in the table. What is the average surface temperature of the stars listed?

1. First find the sum of the data. Add the numbers in the list.

```
  7,200
  6,100
  6,000
  6,550
  7,350
  6,800
  7,500
+ 6,300
-------
 53,800
```

2. Then divide the sum (53,800) by the number of addends (8).

```
     6,725
8 ) 53,800
  - 48
    --
     58
   - 56
     --
      20
    - 16
      --
       40
     - 40
       --
        0
```

3. 53,800 ÷ 8 = 6,725
The average surface temperature of these eight blue-white stars is 6,725°F.

Using a Tape Measure or Ruler

Tape measures, metersticks, and rulers are tools for measuring length. Scientists use units such as kilometers, meters, centimeters, and millimeters when making length measurements.

Use a Meterstick

1. Work with a partner to find the height of your reach. Stand facing a chalkboard. Reach up as high as you can with one hand.

2. Have your partner use chalk to mark the chalkboard at the highest point of your reach.

3. Use a meterstick to measure your reach to the nearest centimeter. Measure from the floor to the chalk mark. Record the height.

Use a Tape Measure

1. Use a tape measure to find the circumference of, or distance around, your partner's head. Wrap the tape around your partner's head.

2. Find the line where the tape begins to wrap over itself.

3. Record the distance around your partner's head to the nearest millimeter.

Measuring Volume

A graduated cylinder, a measuring cup, and a beaker are used to measure volume. Volume is the amount of space something takes up. Most of the containers that scientists use to measure volume have a scale marked in milliliters (mL).

▲ This measuring cup has marks for each 25 mL.

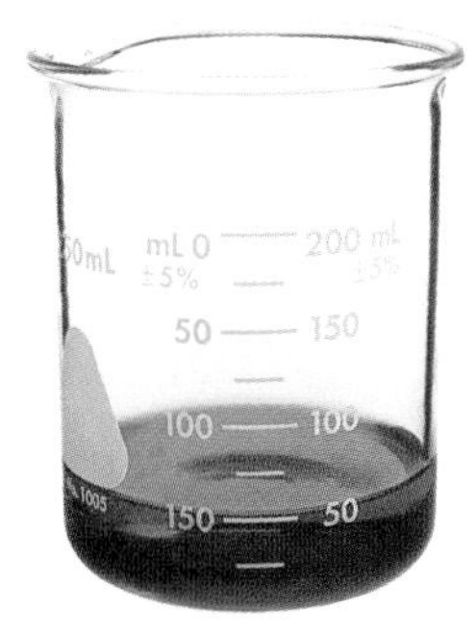

▲ This beaker has marks for each 50 mL.

▲ This graduated cylinder has marks for every 1 mL.

Measure the Volume of a Liquid

1. Measure the volume of some juice. Pour the juice into a measuring container.

2. Move your head so that your eyes are level with the top of the juice. Read the scale line that is closest to the surface of the juice. If the surface of the juice is curved up on the sides, look at the lowest point of the curve.

3. Read the measurement on the scale. You can estimate the value between two lines on the scale to obtain a more accurate measurement.

The bottom of the curve is at 35 mL.

Using a Thermometer

A thermometer is used to measure temperature. When the liquid in the tube of a thermometer gets warmer, it expands and moves farther up the tube. Different scales can be used to measure temperature, but scientists usually use the Celsius scale.

Measure the Temperature of a Liquid

1. Half fill a cup with water or another liquid.

2. Hold the thermometer so that the bulb is in the center of the liquid. Be sure that there are no bright lights or direct sunlight shining on the bulb.

3. Wait until you see the liquid in the tube of the thermometer stop moving. Read the scale line that is closest to the top of the liquid in the tube. The thermometer shown reads 22°C (about 71°F).

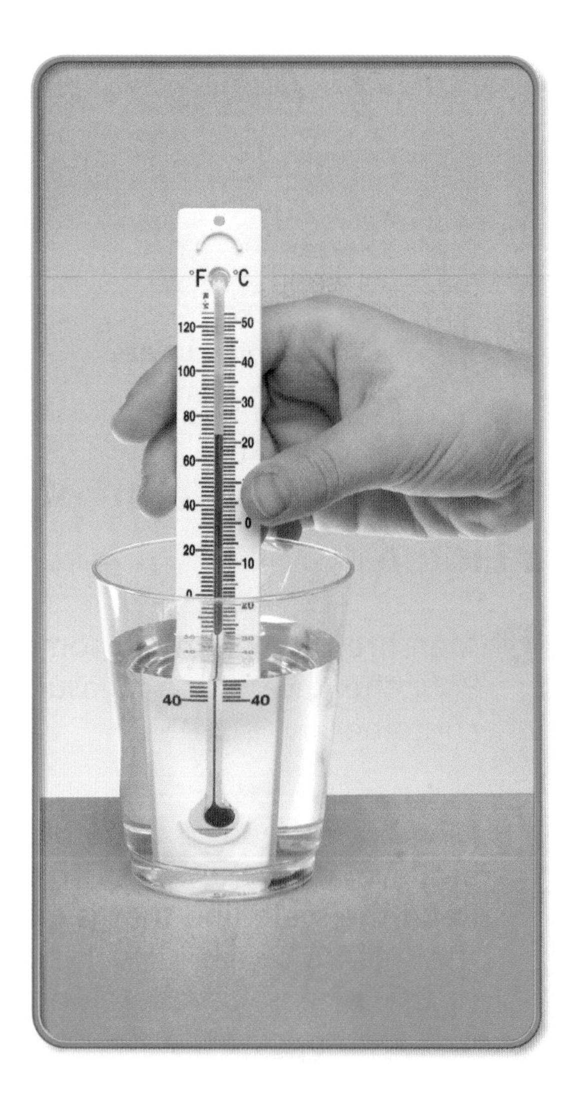

Using a Balance

A balance is used to measure mass. Mass is the amount of matter in an object. To find the mass of an object, place the object in the left pan of the balance. Place standard masses in the right pan.

Measure the Mass of a Ball

1. Check that the empty pans are balanced, or level with each other. When balanced, the pointer on the base should be on the middle mark. If it needs to be adjusted, move the slider on the back of the balance a little to the left or right.

2. Place a ball in the left pan. Then add standard masses, one at a time, to the right pan. When the pointer is at the middle mark again, each pan is holding the same amount of matter, and the same mass.

3. Each standard mass is marked to show its number of grams. Add the number of grams marked on the masses in the pan. The total is the mass of the ball in grams.

Using an Equation or Formula

Equations and formulas can help you to determine measurements that are not easily made.

Use the Diameter of a Circle to Find Its Circumference

1 Find the circumference of a circle that has a diameter of 10 cm. To determine the circumference of a circle, use the formula below.

$C = \pi d$

$C = 3.14 \times 10$ cm

$C = 31.4$ cm

The circumference of this circle is 31.4 cm.

π is the symbol for pi. Always use 3.14 as the value for π, unless another value for pi is given.

10 cm

The circumference (C) is a measure of the distance around a circle.

The diameter (d) of a circle is a line segment that passes through the center of the circle and connects two points on the circle.

Use Rate and Time to Determine Distance

2 Suppose an aircraft travels at 772 km/h for 2.5 hours. How many kilometers does the aircraft travel during that time? To determine distance traveled, use the distance formula below.

$d = rt$

$d = 772 \times 2.5$ km

$d = 1{,}930$ km

The aircraft travels 1,930 km in 2.5 hours.

d = distance

r = rate, or the speed at which the aircraft is traveling.

t = the length of time traveled

Making a Chart to Organize Data

A chart can help you record, compare, or classify information.

Organize Properties of Elements

Suppose you collected the data shown at the right. The data presents properties of silver, gold, lead, and iron.

You could organize this information in a chart by classifying the physical properties of each element.

My Data

Silver (Ag) has a density of 10.5 g/cm^3. It melts at 961°C and boils at 2,212°C. It is used in dentistry and to make jewelry and electronic conductors.

Gold melts at 1,064°C and boils at 2,966°C. Its chemical symbol is Au. It has a density of 19.3 g/cm^3 and is used for jewelry, in coins, and in dentistry.

The melting point of lead (Pb) is 328°C. The boiling point is 1,740°C. It has a density of 11.3 g/cm^3. Some uses for lead are in storage batteries, paints, and dyes.

Iron (Fe) has a density of 7.9 g/cm^3. It will melt at 1,535°C and boil at 3,000°C. It is used for building materials, in manufacturing, and as a dietary supplement.

Create categories that describe the information you have found.

Give the chart a title that describes what is listed in it.

Make sure the information is listed accurately in each column.

Properties of Some Elements

Element	Symbol	Density g/cm^3	Melting Point (°C)	Boiling Point (°C)	Some Uses
Silver	Ag	10.5	961	2,212	jewelry, dentistry, electric conductors
Gold	Au	19.3	1,064	2,966	jewelry, dentistry, coins
Lead	Pb	11.3	328	1,740	storage batteries, paints, dyes
Iron	Fe	7.9	1,535	3,000	building materials, manufacturing, dietary supplement

Reading a Circle Graph

A circle graph shows the whole divided into parts. You can use a circle graph to compare parts to each other or to compare parts to the whole.

Read a Circle Graph of Land Area

The whole circle represents the approximate land area of all of the continents on Earth. The number on each wedge indicates the land area of each continent. From the graph you can determine that the land area of North America is 16% × 148,000,000 km^2, or about 24 million square kilometers.

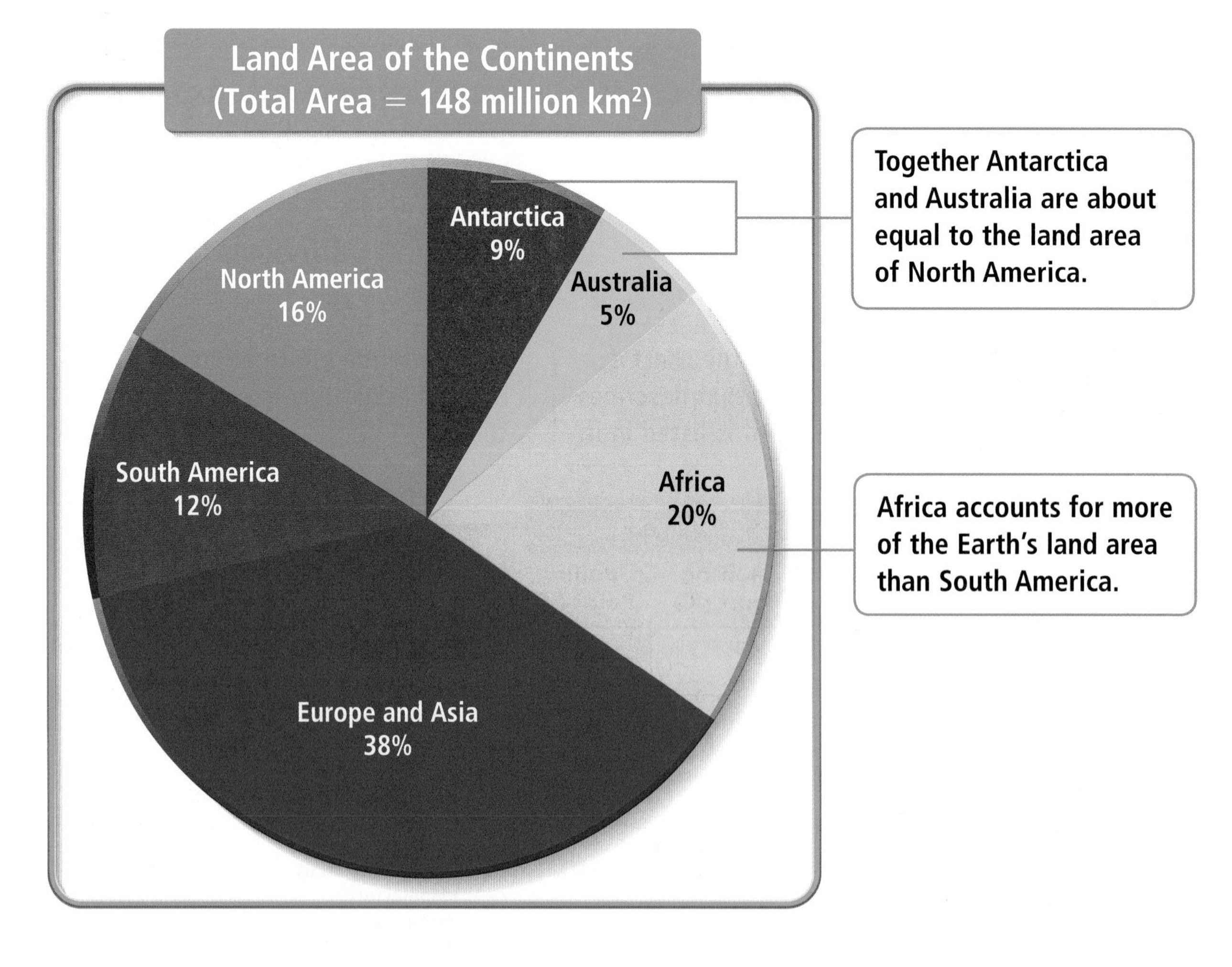

Making a Line Graph

A line graph is a way to show continuous change over time. You can use the information from a table to make a line graph.

Dallas-Fort Worth Airport Temperature	
Hour	**Temp. (°C)**
6 A.M.	22
7 A.M.	24
8 A.M.	25
9 A.M.	26
10 A.M.	27
11 A.M.	29
12 noon	31
1 P.M.	32
2 P.M.	33
3 P.M.	34
4 P.M.	35
5 P.M.	35
6 P.M.	34

Make a Line Graph of Temperatures

The table shows temperature readings over a 12-hour period at the Dallas-Fort Worth Airport in Texas. This data can also be displayed in a line graph that shows temperature change over time.

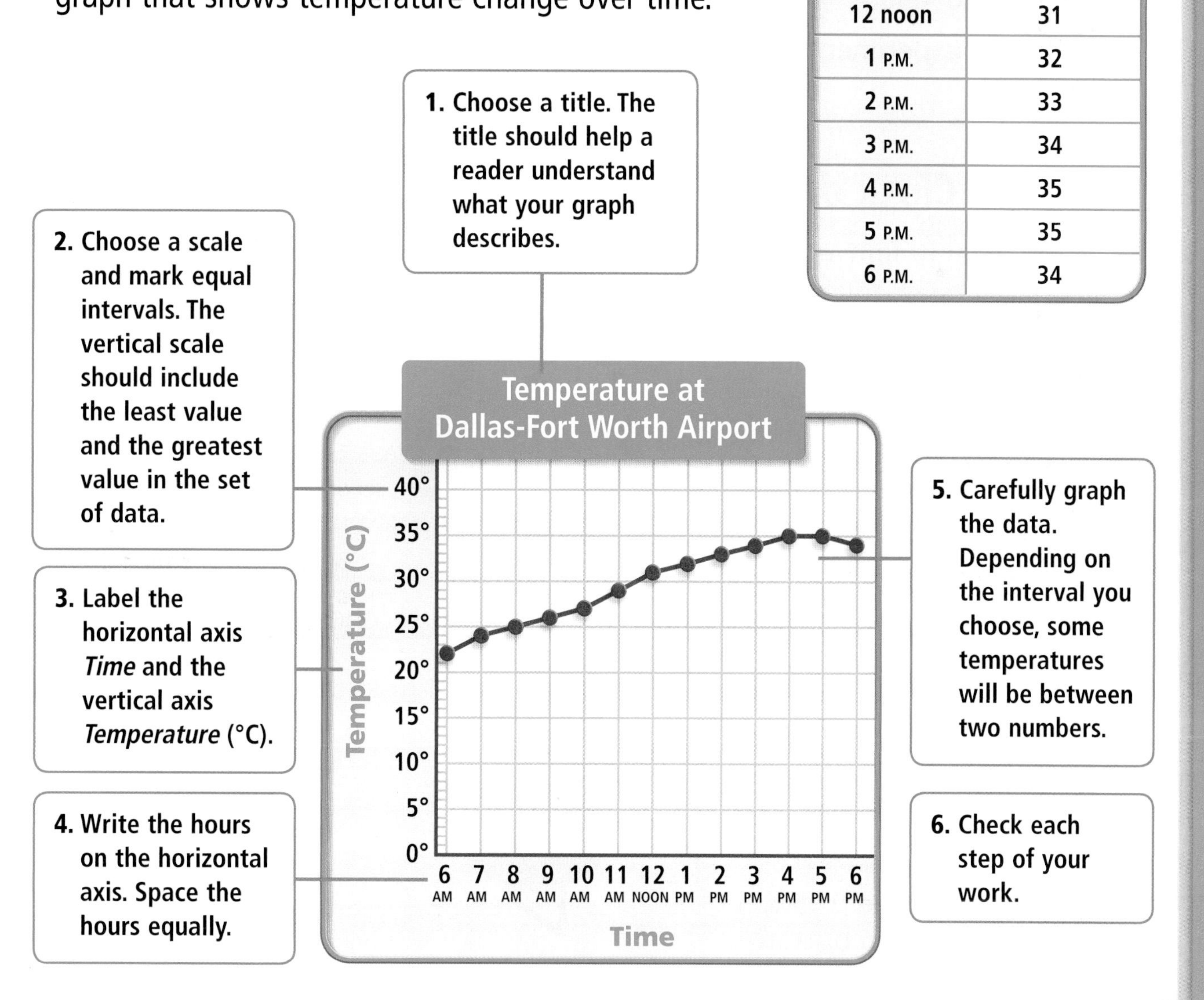

Measuring Elapsed Time

Sometimes you may need to find out how much time has passed, or elapsed. A clock is often used to find elapsed time. You can also change units and add or subtract to find out how much time has passed.

Using a Clock to Find Elapsed Minutes

You need to time an experiment for 20 minutes. It is 1:30.

- Start at 1:30.
- Count ahead 20 minutes, by fives to 1:50.
- Stop the experiment at 1:50.

Using a Clock or Stopwatch to Find Elapsed Seconds

You need to time an experiment for 15 seconds. You can use a second hand on a clock.

 Wait until the second hand is on a number. Then start the experiment.

 Stop the experiment when 15 seconds have passed.

You can also use a stopwatch to figure out elapsed seconds.

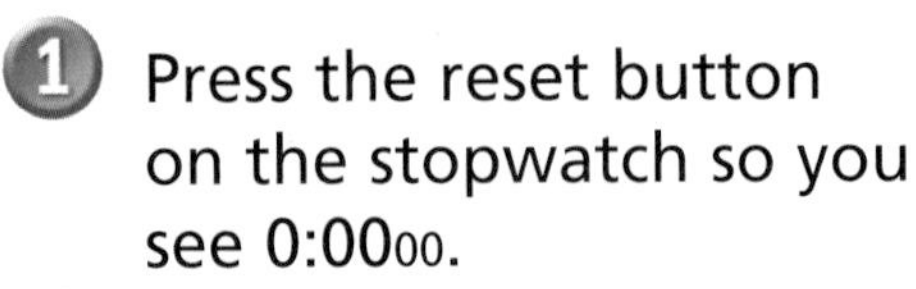

1. Press the reset button on the stopwatch so you see 0:00oo.

2. Press the start button to begin.
3. When you see 0:15oo, press the stop button on the watch.

Changing Units and Then Adding or Subtracting to Find Elapsed Time

If you know how to change units of time, you can use addition and subtraction to find elapsed time.

1. To change from a larger unit to a smaller unit, multiply.

   2 d = ■ h

   $2 \times 24 = 48$

   2 d = 48 h

2. To change from a smaller unit to a larger unit, divide.

   78 wk = ■ yr

   $78 \div 52 = 1\frac{1}{2}$

   78 wk = $1\frac{1}{2}$ yr

Another Example

Suppose it took juice in an ice-pop mold from 6:40 A.M. until 10:15 A.M. to freeze. How long did it take for the juice to freeze? To find out, subtract.

9 h	75 min
~~10 h~~	~~15 min~~
− 6 h	40 min
3 h	35 min

Rename 10 hr 15 min as 9 h 75 min, since 1 hr = 60 min.

Units of Time
60 seconds (s) = 1 minute (min)
60 minutes = 1 hour (hr)
24 hours = 1 day (d)
7 days = 1 week (wk)
52 weeks = 1 year (yr)

You can also add to find elapsed time.

3 h	30 min	14 s
+ 1 h	40 min	45 s
4 h	70 min	59 s = 5 h 10 min 59 s

Measurements

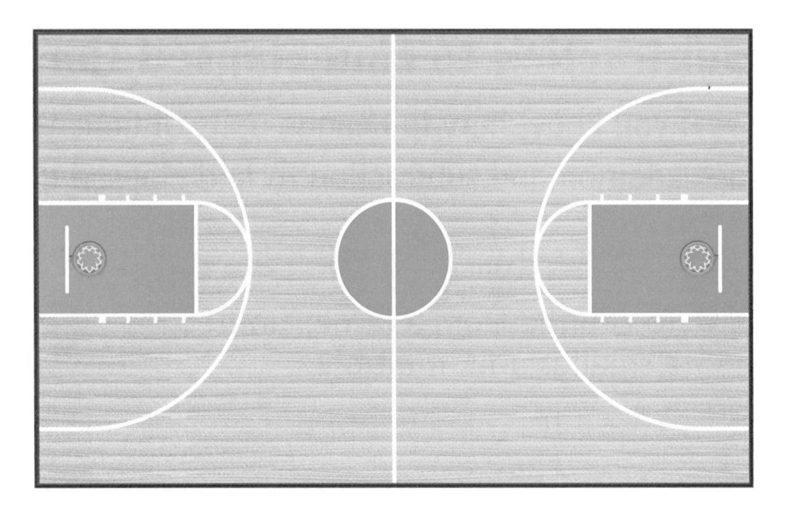

Volume
1 L of sports drink is a little more than 1 qt.

Area
A basketball court covers about 4,700 ft^2. It covers about 435 m^2.

Metric Measures

Temperature

- Ice melts at 0 degrees Celsius (°C)
- Water freezes at 0°C
- Water boils at 100°C

Length and Distance

- 1,000 meters (m) = 1 kilometer (km)
- 100 centimeters (cm) = 1 m
- 10 millimeters (mm) = 1 cm

Force

- 1 newton (N) = 1 kilogram × 1 (meter/second) per second

Volume

- 1 cubic meter (m^3) = 1 m × 1 m × 1 m
- 1 cubic centimeter (cm^3) = 1 cm × 1 cm × 1 cm
- 1 liter (L) = 1,000 milliliters (mL)
- 1 cm^3 = 1 mL

Area

- 1 square kilometer (km^2) = 1 km × 1 km
- 1 hectare = 10,000 m^2

Mass

- 1,000 grams (g) = 1 kilogram (kg)
- 1,000 milligrams (mg) = 1 g

Temperature
The temperature at an indoor basketball game might be 27°C, which is 80°F.

Length/Distance
A basketball rim is about 10 ft high, or a little more than 3 m from the floor.

Customary Measures

Temperature

- Ice melts at 32 degrees Fahrenheit (°F)
- Water freezes at 32°F
- Water boils at 212°F

Length and Distance

- 12 inches (in.) = 1 foot (ft)
- 3 ft = 1 yard (yd)
- 5,280 ft = 1 mile (mi)

Weight

- 16 ounces (oz) = 1 pound (lb)
- 2,000 pounds = 1 ton (T)

Volume of Fluids

- 8 fluid ounces (fl oz) = 1 cup (c)
- 2 c = 1 pint (pt)
- 2 pt = 1 quart (qt)
- 4 qt = 1 gallon (gal)

Metric and Customary Rates

- km/h = kilometers per hour
- m/s = meters per second
- mph = miles per hour

Health and Fitness Handbook

Who is in charge of your health? You! Doctors, nurses, your parents or guardian, and teachers can all help you stay healthy. However, it's up to you to make healthful choices. What are some healthful choices you can make? In this section you'll learn:

- how to keep your body systems strong and healthy
- how to choose healthful foods
- how to exercise your heart and lungs every day
- how to be prepared for emergencies
- the benefits of avoiding alcohol, tobacco, and other drugs

The Muscular System

Your muscular system has three types of muscles.

- *Skeletal muscles* pull on bones to move them. You use them whenever you move your body.
- *Cardiac muscles* make up the walls of your heart and keep it beating.
- *Smooth muscles* line the blood vessels, the stomach, and other organs.

Most skeletal muscles are *voluntary muscles.* You can control them. Cardiac and smooth muscles are *involuntary muscles.* They work without you even having to think about them!

Many skeletal muscles work in pairs. When the biceps muscle in your arm contracts (gets shorter), the triceps muscle relaxes (gets longer). As a result, the elbow bends. How would the muscles work together to straighten the arm?

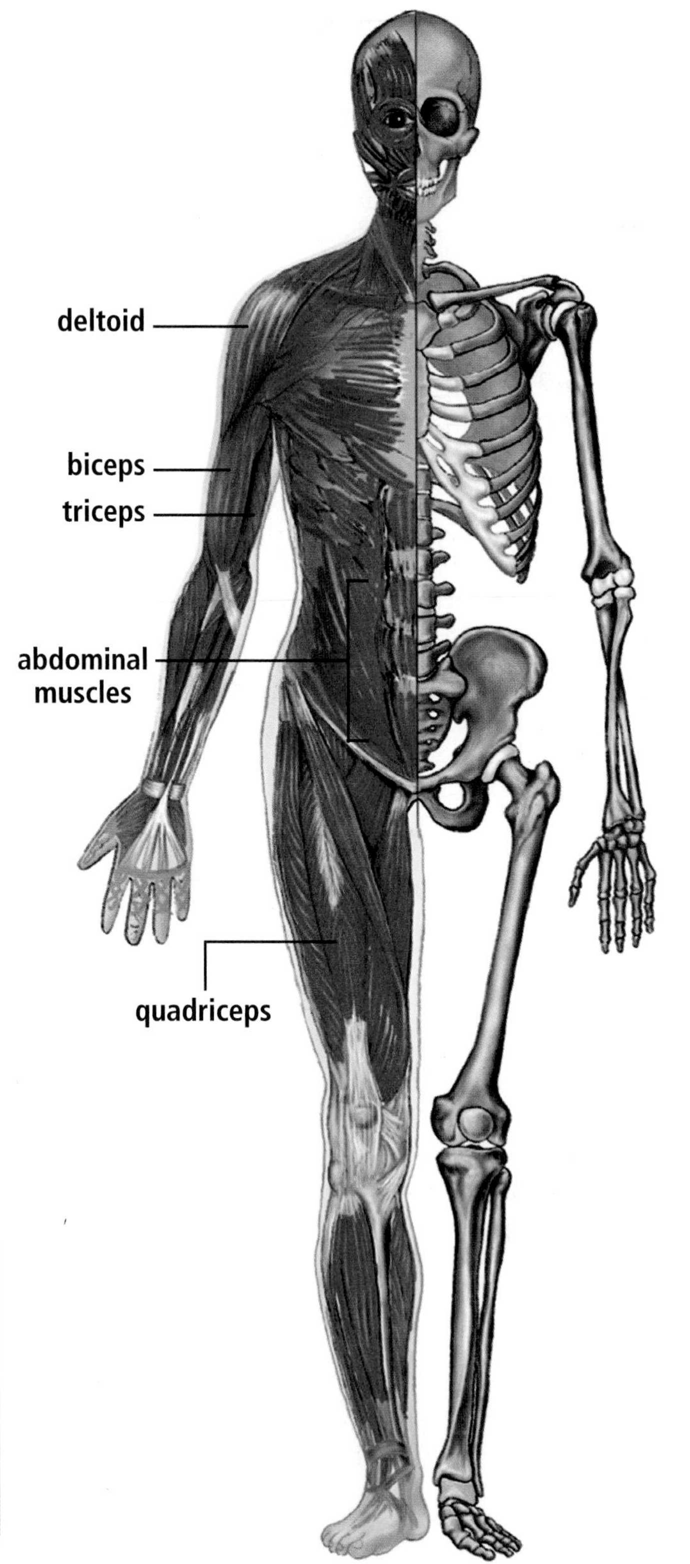

FACTS

- Your muscles receive about 50 messages from your brain every second.
- You have more than 650 muscles.

The Skeletal System

Joints connect bones. If you had no joints, you could not bend or move. Each type of joint allows different kinds of movement. Your elbow has a hinge joint. The arm bends only one way at the elbow. Think about your shoulder. It has a ball-and-socket joint. What movement does it allow?

Your skeletal system gives your body strength and support. It works with your muscular system to move body parts. Your bones also protect your organs.

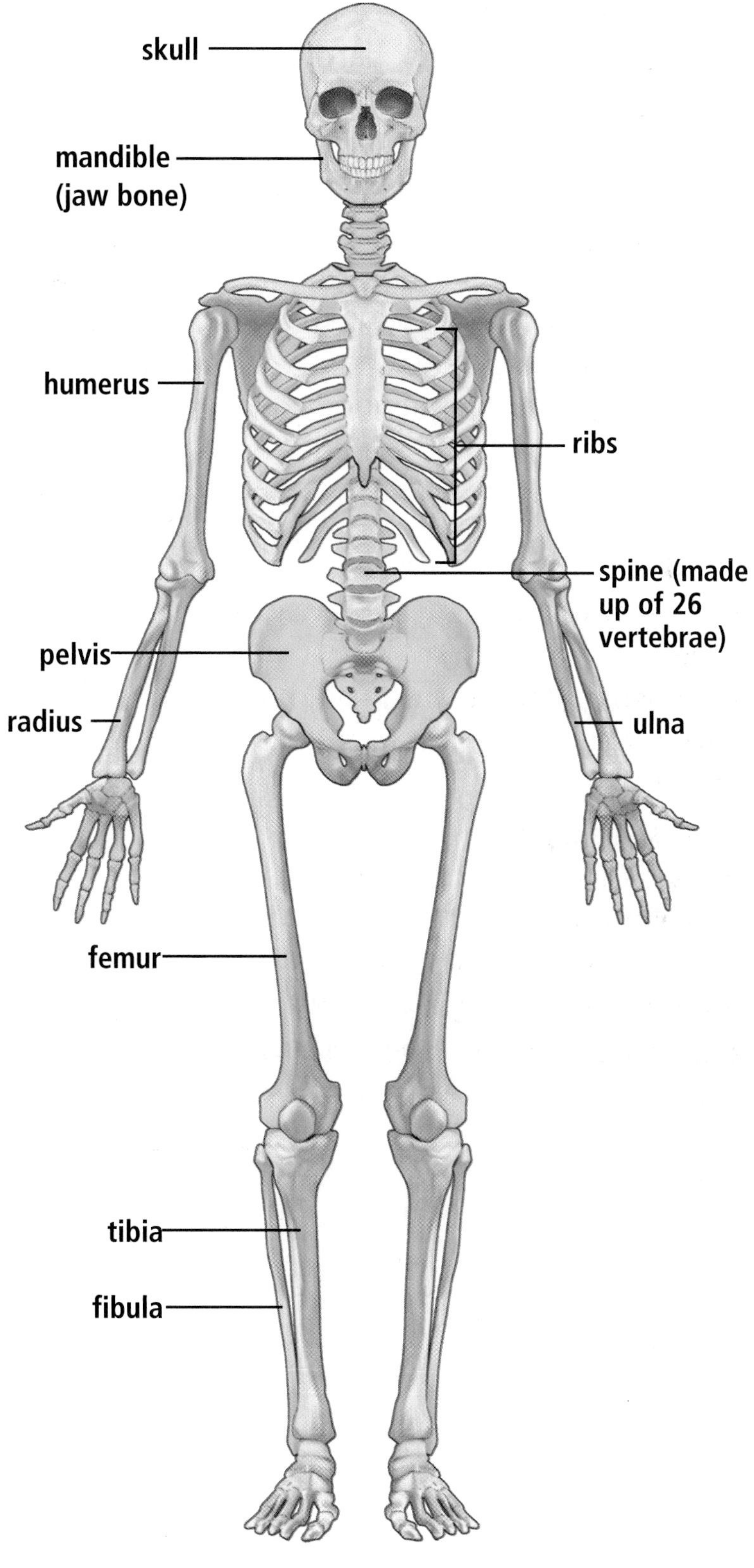

FACTS

- You have 206 bones in your body. More than half of them are found in your hands and feet!
- Your bones come in all shapes and sizes. There's even a bone in your ear shaped like a hammer!

Exercise Your Heart and Lungs

Exercise that makes your heart and lungs work hard is called aerobic exercise. *Aerobic* means "with oxygen." Any kind of steady exercise that raises your heart and breathing rates is aerobic exercise. Jogging, swimming, bicycling, and playing soccer are all good ways to get aerobic exercise.

Five steps toward a great aerobic workout.

1. **Choose your activity.** Pick an activity you enjoy. Do you like exercising with others? Basketball might be a good choice. Do you like exercising to music? Maybe you'd like dancing!

2. **Get the equipment you need.** Make sure you have the right clothes and shoes for your activity. Wear any safety gear you need. Your clothes and safety gear should fit correctly. Ask a parent, guardian, or physical education teacher for help.

3. **Warm up.** Do gentle activity such as walking for five minutes. Then stretch your muscles.

4. **Exercise.** It's best to exercise for at least 20 minutes. Exercise at a level that makes your heart and lungs work. Stop right away if you are injured.

5. **Cool down.** Exercise at a lower level for five to ten minutes to let your heart and breathing rates come back down. Then stretch your muscles again.

Food Labels

The United States Food and Drug Administration (FDA) requires most companies that sell food to label their packages. The facts shown on food labels can help you make smart food choices. Food labels list the ingredients in the food. They are in order by weight. This means that the food contains the most of the first ingredient listed. The label also tells you the name of the company that makes the food and the total weight or volume of the food in the package.

Food labels also include the Nutrition Facts panel. The panel on the right is for a can of chicken soup.

Nutrition Facts
Serving Size 1 cup (246g)
Servings Per Container About 2

Amount Per Serving	
Calories 110	Calories from Fat 20
	% Daily Value*
Total Fat 2.5g	**4%**
Saturated Fat 0.5g	**3%**
Cholesterol 25mg	**8%**
Sodium 960mg	**40%**
Total Carbohydrate 15g	**5%**
Dietary Fiber 1g	**5%**
Sugars 2g	
Protein 9g	
Vitamin A 30% •	Vitamin C 0%
Calcium 2% •	Iron 4%

*Percent Daily Values are based on a 2,000 calorie diet.

▲ **What nutrients are in the food you eat? Read the Nutrition Facts panel to find out! Calories measure the energy in food.**

Get Enough Nutrients

- Carbohydrates provide energy. Fiber helps the digestive system.
- Your body uses protein for growth and development.
- Vitamins and minerals are important for many body functions.

FACTS

Limit Some Nutrients

- A healthful diet includes a limited amount of fat. Saturated fats and trans fats can increase the risk of heart disease. Cholesterol is a fat-like substance that can clog arteries.
- Too much sodium can increase the risk of high blood pressure.

Emergency Safety

Earthquakes, hurricanes, and tornadoes are all examples of natural disasters. You can plan ahead so you know what to do when a disaster happens.

Plan Ahead

You might not have fresh running water or electricity during a natural disaster. Here are some items you might want to have on hand.

- flashlights with batteries
- candles or lanterns with matches
- at least two gallons of fresh water
- canned or packaged food that does not need to be cooked
- radio with batteries
- first-aid kit

What To Do

Earthquake Get under something solid like a desk or doorway. Stay away from windows. Also stay away from anything that might fall on you. If you are outdoors, get to a wide open area.

Hurricane If there is some warning that a hurricane is coming, you may be told to evacuate. Tape all windows. Your parents or guardian will probably shut off the gas, water, and electricity.

Tornado If you are inside, go to a storm shelter or basement if you can. If there is no basement, go to an inside room with no windows. If you are outside, lie down in a low area and cover your head.

Tobacco, Alcohol, and Other Drugs

A drug is any substance, other than food, that changes how the body works. Drugs are swallowed, smoked, inhaled, or injected.

Helpful Drugs

Some drugs are helpful. Medicines can treat diseases and relieve pain. Drugs people can buy without a doctor's order are called *over-the-counter medicines.* Medicines that need a doctor's order are called *prescription medicines.*

Medicines can harm you if you use them incorrectly. Only take medicine when your parent, guardian, or doctor tells you to. Follow your doctor's instructions or the instructions printed on the package.

Harmful Drugs

Some drugs can harm your health.

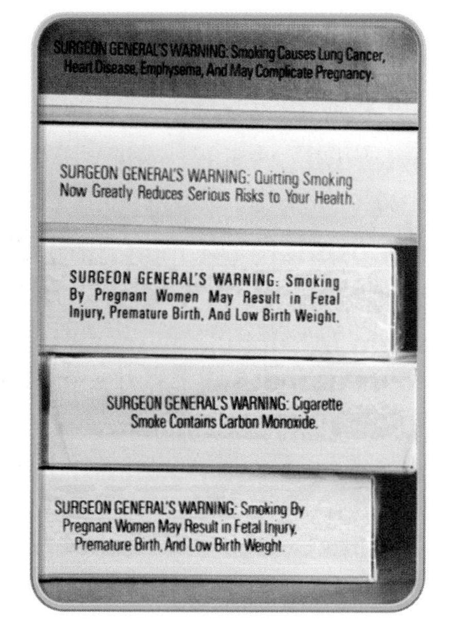

Tobacco is a leaf that is smoked, sniffed, or chewed. Tobacco contains many harmful substances, including nicotine which speeds up the heart. Tobacco is addictive. This means that it is very hard to stop using tobacco once a person starts. Tobacco increases your risk of heart disease and lung disease.

Alcohol is a drug found in drinks such as beer and wine. Alcohol slows brain activity and muscle activity. Heavy drinking can lead to addiction and can damage the liver and other organs. People who drink alcohol are more likely to get into accidents.

Illegal drugs include marijuana, cocaine, ecstasy, LSD, and amphetamines. These drugs can cause serious physical, emotional, and social problems.

acceleration (ak sehl uh RAY shuhn), change in velocity (F9)

acquired trait (uh KWYRD trayt), characteristic that an organism develops after it is born (A84)

adaptation (ad ap TAY shuhn), a trait or characteristic that helps an organism survive in its environment (A102, B40)

air mass (air mas), huge volume of air responsible for types of weather (D18)

analyze data (AN uh lyz DAY tuh), to look for patterns in collected information that lead to making logical inferences, predictions, and hypotheses

angiosperms (AN jee uh spurmz), plants with seeds covered by protective fruits (A70)

asexual reproduction (ay SEHK shoo uhl ree pruh DUHK shuhn), production of offspring from only one parent (A96)

ask questions (ask KWEHS chunz), to state questions orally or in writing to find out how or why something happens

asteroid (AS tuh royd), small, rocky object that orbits the Sun (D58)

atmosphere (AT muh sfihr), mixture of gases that surrounds Earth (D16)

atom (AT uhm), the smallest particle of an element that still has the properties of that element (E6)

autumnal equinox (aw TUHM nuhl EE kwuh nahks), September 22 or 23, when the number of hours of daylight and darkness are the same (D34)

axis (AK sihs), imaginary line that goes through the center of Earth from the North Pole to the South Pole (D32)

biome (BY ohm), large group of similar ecosystems (B12)

boiling point (BOY lihng point), temperature at which a substance changes from a liquid to a gas (E45)

cell (sehl), the basic structural unit of a living thing (A6)

chemical change (KEHM ih kuhl chaynj), change in matter that results in new substances being formed (E53)

chemical formula (KEHM ih kuhl FAWR myuh luh), a shorthand way to describe the chemical makeup of a compound (E29)

chemical property (KEHM ih kuhl PRAHP uhr tee), ability of a material to change its chemical makeup (E43)

chemical reaction (KEHM ih kuhl ree AK shuhn), a process in which one or more substances are changed into one or more different substances, or a specific example of one or more chemical changes (E28, E53)

chemical symbol (KEHM ih kuhl SIHM buhl), a letter or letters that abbreviates an element's name (E16)

chlorophyll (KLAWR uh fihl), the green pigment in leaves that collects energy from sunlight (A51)

chloroplasts (KLAWR uh plastz), plant organelles inside which photosynthesis takes place (A51)

chromosome (KROH muh sohm), short, thick coil of DNA (A86)

cilia (SIHL ee uh), small structures that look like hairs (A16)

classification (klas uh fih KAY shuhn), process of sorting things based on similarities and differences (A24)

classify (KLAS uh fy), to sort objects into groups according to their properties to order objects according to a pattern

climate (KLY miht), normal pattern of weather that occurs in an area over a long period of time (B12, D7)

collaborate (kuh LAB uh rayt), to work as a team with others to collect and share data, observations, findings, and ideas

comet (KAHM iht), small orbiting body made of dust, ice, and frozen gases (D59)

communicate (kah MYOO nuh kayt), to explain procedures or share information, data, or findings with others through written or spoken words, actions, graphs, charts, tables, diagrams, or sketches

community (kuh MYOO nih tee), group of living things of different species found in an ecosystem (B7)

compare (kuhm PAIR), to observe and tell how objects or events are alike or different

compound (KAHM pownd), a substance that is made up of two or more elements that are chemically combined (E26)

condensation (kahn dehn SAY shuhn), change of state from a gas to a liquid as energy is removed (E85)

conduction (kuhn DUHK shuhn), transfer of thermal energy between two substances or between two parts of the same substance (F88)

conductivity (kuhn duhk TIHV ih tee), ability to carry energy (E46)

conductor (kuhn DUHK tuhr), material that easily transfers thermal energy or electricity (F92)

conservation (kahn sur VAY shuhn), efficient use of resources (C78)

consumer (kuhn SOO muhr), organism that gets energy by eating food, not producing it (B24)

contour lines (KAHN tur lynz), lines on a topographic map that indicate areas with the same elevation, or height above sea level (C10)

convection (kuhn VEHK shuhn), transfer of thermal energy by the flow of liquids or gases (F89)

core (kohr), Earth's innermost structure (C41)

crust (kruhst), the thin, rocky outer layer of Earth that makes up the continents and the ocean floor (C7, C40)

density (DEHN sih tee), mass per unit volume of a substance (E44)

deposition (dehp uh ZIHSH uhn), [1] constructive force in which sediments that have been moved from one place are dropped or released in another place, or [2] change of state from a gas to a solid (C24, E86)

desert (DEHZ uhrt), a very dry area (B14)

diffusion (dih FYOO zhuhn), movement of particles from an area of higher concentration to an area of lower concentration (A17)

DNA molecule found in the nucleus of a cell and shaped like a double helix; associated with the transfer of genetic information (A86)

dome mountains (dohm MOWN tuhnz), mountains that form when magma pushes up on Earth's crust but does not break through (C64)

dominant trait (DAHM uh nuhnt trayt), trait that is expressed when an organism receives genes for two different forms of a trait (A99)

E

earthquake (URTH kwayk), violent shaking of Earth's crust as built-up energy is released (C54)

ecosystem (EHK oh sihs tuhm), all the living and nonliving things that interact with one another in a given area (B6)

El Niño (ehl NEE nyo), periodic change in the direction of warm ocean currents across the Pacific Ocean (D10)

electric cell (ih LEHK trihk sehl), device that uses a chemical reaction to produce electricity

electric circuit (ih LEHK trihk SUR kiht), pathway for an electric current (F112)

electric current (ih LEHK trihk KUR uhnt), continuous flow of electric charge along a pathway

electric generator (ih LEHK trihk JEHN uh ray tuhr), device that converts kinetic energy to electricity (F107)

electric motor (ih LEHK trihk MOH tuhr), device that converts electrical energy into kinetic energy (F126)

electromagnet (ih lehk troh MAG niht), a magnet that is powered by electricity (F32)

electron (ih LEHK trahn), a particle in an atom that has a negative charge (E7)

element (EHL uh muhnt), a substance that cannot be broken down into other substances (E6)

endangered species (ehn DAYN juhrd SPEE sheez), a species close to becoming extinct (B59)

energy (EHN uhr jee), ability to do work (F44)

epicenter (EHP ih sehn tuhr), point on Earth's surface directly above the focus of an earthquake (C54)

erosion (ih ROH zhuhn), destructive force in which pieces of rock are moved by water, wind, or moving ice (C16)

experiment (ihks SPEHR uh muhnt), to investigate and collect data that either supports a hypothesis or shows that it is false while controlling variables and changing only one part of an experimental setup at a time

extinction (ihk STIHNGK shuhn), when all members of a species die out (B51)

fault (fawlt), crack in Earth's crust along which movement takes place (C52)

fault-block mountains (fahwlt blahk MOWN tuhnz), mountains that form along fault lines where blocks of rock fall, are thrust up, or slide (C63)

flagellum (fluh JEHL uhm), whip-like tail that helps single-celled organisms move by spinning like a propeller (A17)

focus (FOH kuhs), point underground where the faulting in an earthquake occurs (C54)

fold mountains (fohld MOWN tuhnz), mountains that form where two plates collide and force layers of rock into folds (C62)

food chain (food chayn), description of how energy in an ecosystem flows from one organism to another (B25)

food web (food wehb), description of all the food chains in an ecosystem (B26)

force (fawrs), push or pull acting on an object (F7)

fossil (FAH suhl), physical remains or traces of a plant or animal that lived long ago (C44)

fossil fuel (FAHS uhl fyool), nonrenewable resource formed from ancient plants and animals (C75)

friction (FRIHK shuhn), force from rubbing (F12)

front (fruhnt), narrow region between two air masses that have different properties (D19)

fungi (FUHN jee), kingdom of living things; its organisms are multicellular, have nuclei, and often feed on decaying matter (A26)

galaxy (GAL uhk see), an enormous system of gases, dust, and stars held together by gravity (D78)

gas (gas), state of matter that has no definite shape or volume (E78)

gene (jeen), short segment of DNA that determines an organism's inherited traits (A87)

grasslands (GRAS landz), land covered by grasses with few trees (B14)

gravity (GRAV ih tee), pulling force between objects (F12)

gymnosperms (JIHM nuh spurmz), plants with seeds that are not covered by protective fruits (A69)

habitat (HAB ih tat), the natural environment where an organism lives (B38)

heat (heet), transfer of thermal energy from warmer areas to cooler areas (F80)

heredity (huh REHD ih tee), genetic transfer of characteristics from parent to offspring (A84)

hybrid (HY brihd), organism that has two different genes for the same trait (A99)

hypothesize (hy PAHTH uh syz), to make an educated guess about why something happens

inertia (ih NUR shuh), resistance to a change in motion (F7)

infer (ihn FUR), to use facts, data, and observations to draw a conclusion about a specific event

inner planets (IHN uhr PLAN ihtz), the four planets of the solar system that are closest to the sun — Mercury, Venus, Earth, and Mars (D64)

insulator (IHN suh lay tuhr), material that does not easily transfer thermal energy or electricity (F92)

invertebrate (ihn VUR tuh briht), animal that has no internal skeleton or bones (A28)

K

kinetic energy (kih NEHT ihk EHN uhr jee), energy of a moving object (F46)

kingdom (KIHNG duhm), largest group of organisms that share traits in common (A24)

life cycle (lyf SY kuhl), sequence of life events beginning with a seed and ending with the next generation of seeds (A68)

light-year (LYT yihr), unit of measurement for distances outside the solar system and equal to about 9.5 trillion km (D75)

liquid (LIHK wihd), state of matter that has a definite volume, but no definite shape (E77)

lithosphere (LIHTH uh sfihr), shell formed from Earth's solid upper mantle and crust (C41)

lunar eclipse (LOO nuhr ih KLIHPS), when Earth passes directly between the Sun and the Moon, casting a shadow on the Moon (D46)

magma (MAG muh), melted rock below Earth's surface; called lava at the surface (C56)

magnitude (MAG nih tood), brightness of a star as perceived from Earth (D75)

mantle (MAN tl), thick layer of Earth's structure just below Earth's crust (C41)

measure (MEHZH uhr), to use a variety of measuring instruments and tools to find the length, distance, volume, mass, or temperature using appropriate units of measurement

mechanical wave (mih KAN ih kuhl wayv), wave that can travel only through matter (F52)

melting (MEHL tihng), change of state from a solid to a liquid as energy is added (E84)

melting point (MEHL tihng point), temperature at which a substance changes from a solid to a liquid (E45)

mesosphere (MEHZ oh sfeer), layer of the atmosphere above the stratosphere and below the thermosphere (D17)

Glossary

metal (MEHT l), any one of the elements located on the left and bottom of the periodic table, which are usually shiny, can be bent or stretched, and conduct electricity (E17)

meteor (MEE tee uhr), chunk of matter that enters Earth's atmosphere and is heated by friction with the air (D60)

meteorites (MEE tee uh rytz), chunks of meteor matter that fall to the ground (D60)

mixture (MIHKS chuhr), physical combination of two or more substances (E60)

molecule (MAHL ih kyool), two or more atoms joined by chemical bonds (E10)

moon phases (moon FAYZ ihz), shapes created by the changing amounts of the visible lighted areas of the Moon (D44)

motion (MOH shuhn), change in an object's position (F6)

mutation (myoo TAY shuhn), change in the genes of an organism (A89)

natural resource (NACH uhr uhl REE sawrs), resource found in nature, such as air, water, minerals, and soil (C74)

neutron (NOO trahn), a particle in the nucleus of an atom that has no charge (E8)

newton (NOOT n), unit to measure force, it is equal to the force required to accelerate a 1 kg mass by 1 m/s^2 (F11)

niche (nihch), the role of an organism in its habitat (B39)

noble gas (NOH buhl gas), any one of the elements located in the far right column of the periodic table, which generally do not combine with other elements to form molecules (E20)

nonmetal (nahn MEHT l), elements that are usually dull, brittle, and do not conduct electricity (E17)

nonrenewable resource (nahn rih NOO uh buhl REE sawrs), resource that is difficult to replace (C75)

nonvascular plant (nahn VAS kyoo luhr plant), a simple plant that lacks true leaves, stems, and roots (A62)

nucleotide (NOO klee uh tyd), basic structural unit of DNA (A87)

nucleus (NOO klee uhs), storehouse of the cell's most important chemical information, or the central core of an atom (A8, E7)

observe (UHB zuhrv), to use the senses and tools to gather or collect information and determine the properties of objects or events

ocean current (OH shuhn KUR uhnt), moving stream of water created by winds pushing against the ocean's surface (D10)

organ (AWR guhn), group of one or more kinds of tissues that work together to perform the same function (A33)

organ system (AWR guhn SIHS tuhm), group of interconnected organs that perform related life functions (A33)

organelle (AWR guh nehl), cell structure that performs specific functions (A8)

osmosis (ahz MOH sihs), type of diffusion in which water passes through a cell membrane (A17)

outer planets (OW tuhr PLAN ihtz), the five planets of the solar system farthest from the Sun—Jupiter, Saturn, Uranus, Neptune, and Pluto (D66)

parallel circuit (PAR uh lehl SUR kiht), circuit where electric current can follow two or more different paths (F115)

penumbra (pih NUHM bruh), large partial shadow in an eclipse (D46)

periodic table (pihr ee AHD ihk TAY buhl), a table that organizes the elements by their properties (E15)

phloem (FLOH ehm), specialized tissue within roots, stems, and leaves that moves materials (A63)

photosynthesis (foh toh SIHN thih sihs), the process by which plants use light energy to convert water and carbon dioxide into sugars and oxygen (A50)

physical change (FIHZ ih kuhl chaynj), change in the size, shape, or state of matter with no new matter being formed (E52)

physical property (FIHZ ih kuhl PRAHP uhr tee), characteristic that can be measured or detected by the senses (E43)

pitch (pihch), perceived highness or lowness of a sound (F56)

planet (PLAN iht), large bodies that revolve around the Sun (D56)

plate tectonics (playt tehk TAHN ihks), theory that giant plates of crust are moving slowly across Earth's surface (C42)

pollination (pahl ih NAY shuhn), process of delivering pollen (male) to the egg (female) in a plant (A69)

pollution (puh LOO shuhn), addition of harmful substances to the environment (B60)

population (pahp yuh LAY shuhn), all the members of the same type of organism living in an ecosystem (B8, B46)

population density (pahp yuh LAY shuhn DEHN sih tee), number of individuals in a population in a given area (B47)

potential energy (puh TEHN shuhl EHN uhr jee), energy stored in an object (F46)

predator (PREHD uh tuhr), animal that hunts and eats other animals (B47)

predict (prih DIHKT), to state what you think will happen based on past experience, observations, patterns, and cause-and-effect relationships

prey (pray), animal that is hunted and eaten by predators (B47)

producer (pruh DOO suhr), organism that makes its own food from raw materials and energy (B24)

protist (PROH tihst), kingdom of living things; its organisms are mostly one-celled but have nuclei and other organelles (A25)

proton (PROH tahn), a particle in the nucleus of an atom that has a positive charge (E8)

protostar (PROH tuh stahr), first stage in the formation of a star (D76)

radiation (ray dee AY shuhn), transfer of thermal energy through electromagnetic waves (F90)

recessive trait (rih SEHS ihv trayt), trait that is not expressed when an organism receives genes for two different forms of a trait (A99)

record data (rih KAWRD DAY tuh), to write, draw, audio record, video record, or photograph to show observations

recycling (ree SY klihng), process of recovering a resource from one item and using it to make another item (C92)

reflection (rih FLEHK shuhn), bouncing of a wave off a material (F66)

refraction (rih FRAK shuhn), changing of the path of a wave as it moves between materials of different densities (F66)

renewable resource (rih NOO uh buhl REE sawrs), resource that is easily replaced or renewed (C76)

research (rih SURCH), to learn more about a subject by looking in books, newspapers, magazines, CD-ROMS, searching the Internet, or asking science experts

residual soil (rih ZIHJ oo uhl soyl), soil formed directly from the bedrock below it (C85)

revolution (rehv uh LOO shuhn), one full trip, or orbit, around the Sun (D33)

scientific inquiry (sy uhn TIH fik IN kwih ree), method scientists use to ask and answer questions about the world around them (S3)

sediment (SEHD uh muhnt), small pieces of rock (C14)

seismic waves (SYZ mihk wayvz), waves of energy sent through Earth's crust when parts of the crust move suddenly (C53)

selective breeding (suh LEHK tihv BREE ding), practice of breeding plants and animals for desirable traits (A100)

semi-metal (SEHM ee meht l), elements that have some properties of metals and some properties of nonmetals (E17)

series circuit (SIHR eez SUR kiht), circuit where only a single path for electricity connects two or more devices (F114)

sexual reproduction (SEHK shoo uhl ree pruh DUHK shuhn), production of offspring by the union of male and female gametes (A98)

simple machine (SIHM puhl muh SHEEN), a machine that has few or no moving parts (F17)

soil (soyl), natural resource made up of small rocks, minerals, water, gases, and organic matter (C84)

soil profile (soyl PROH fyl), all of the soil horizons, or layers, in a soil sample (C86)

solar eclipse (SOH luhr ih KLIHPS), when the Moon passes directly between the Sun and Earth, casting a shadow on Earth (D46)

solar system (SOH luhr SIHS tuhm), the Sun and all bodies that revolve around it (D56)

solid (SAHL ihd), state of matter that has a definite shape and volume (E76)

solubility (sahl yuh BIHL ih tee), measure of how much of one substance can dissolve in another substance (E46)

solute (SAHL yoot), substance that is dissolved in a solution (E62)

solution (suh LOO shuhn), mixture of two or more substances that are evenly distributed throughout the mixture (E62)

solvent (SAHL vuhnt), substance that dissolves the solute in a solution (E62)

speed (speed), measure of the distance an object moves in a given unit of time (F8)

spores (spawrz), reproductive structures found in fungi and simple plants (A68)

stars (stahrz), giant sphere of glowing gases (D74)

state of matter (stayt uhv MAT uhr), physical form that matter takes; gas, liquid, and solid (E74)

static electricity (STAT ihk ih lehk TRIHS ih tee), electrical force between nonmoving electric charges (F104)

stomata (STOH muh tuh), small openings through which gases move in and out of leaves (A52)

stratosphere (STRA tuh sfeer), layer of the atmosphere above the troposphere and below the mesosphere (D17)

sublimation (suhb luh MAY shuhn), change of state from a solid to a gas (E86)

subsoil (SUHB soyl), layer of soil beneath the topsoil (C86)

summer solstice (SUHM uhr SAHL stihs), June 21 or 22, the longest day of the year in the Northern Hemisphere (D34)

switch (swihch), movable section of a circuit that can open or close a path for electricity (F113)

symbiosis (sihm bee OH sihs), close, long-lasting relationship between species (B42)

taiga (TY guh), area that has long, severe winters and short, cool summers (B15)

technology (tehk NAH luh jee), tools, things built with tools, or methods used to accomplish a practical purpose (S11)

temperate forests forests that experience four distinct seasons: summer, fall, winter, and spring (B13)

temperature (TEHM puhr uh chur), measure of the average kinetic energy of the particles that make up a substance (F78)

thermal energy total kinetic energy of the particles of a substance (F78)

thermal expansion (THUHR muhl ihk SPAN shuhn), increase in size of a substance due to a change in temperature (E87)

thermosphere (THUHR muh sfeer), the outermost layer of the atmosphere, above the mesosphere (D17)

threatened species (THREHT nd SPEE sheez), a species close to becoming endangered (B59)

tissue (TIHSH oo), group of one or more kinds of specialized cells that perform the same function (A33)

topographic map map that shows the shape of surface features and their elevations above sea level (C10)

topsoil uppermost layer of soil (C86)

transpiration (tran spuh RAY shuhn), evaporation through the leaves of a plant (A64)

transported soil (trans PAWRT ihd soyl), soil that has been carried from one place to another by erosion (C85)

tropical rain forests forests in regions that are very hot and very rainy (B13)

troposphere (TROH puh sfihr), layer of Earth's atmosphere closest to Earth's surface and containing about three-quarters of the atmosphere's gases (D17)

tundra Earth's coldest biome (B15)

umbra (UHM bruh), small, dark shadow in an eclipse (D46)

use variables (yooz VAIR ee uh buhlz), to keep all conditions in an experiment the same except for the variable, or the condition that is being tested

vaporization (vay puh rih ZAY shuhn), change of state from a liquid to a gas as energy is added (E85)

vascular plant a plant with specialized tissues and organs for transporting materials (A63)

velocity (vuh LAHS ih tee), measure of speed and direction (F8)

vernal equinox (VUR nuhl EE kwuh nahks), March 20 or 21, when the number of hours of daylight and darkness are the same (D34)

vertebrate (VUR tuh briht), animal that has an internal skeleton or backbone (A26)

vibration (vy BRAY shuhn), rapid back-and-forth movement (F54)

visible light portion of the electromagnetic spectrum humans can see (F65)

voltage (VOHL tihj), measure of the force that moves electrons (F127)

volume (VAHL yoom), loudness of a sound, or the space an object takes up (F57)

weathering destructive force that breaks down rocks into smaller pieces (C14)

winter solstice (WIHN tuhr SAHL stihs), December 21 or 22, the shortest day of the year in the Northern Hemisphere (D34)

work (wurk), result of a force moving an object a certain distance (F16)

xylem (ZY luhm), specialized plant tissue that moves materials (A63)

C

D

Index

E

N

O

R

W

Literature:

Excerpt from *The River of Grass* from *Everglades: Buffalo Tiger and the River of Grass,* by Peter Lourie. Copyright © 1994 by Peter Lourie. Reprinted by permission of Caroline House, Boyds Mills Press, Inc.
Some Rivers from *Sawgrass Poems: A View From the Everglades,* by Frank Asch. Copyright © 1996 by Frank Asch. Reprinted by permission of Harcourt, Inc. This material may not be reproduced in any form or by any means without the prior written permission of the publisher.
Excerpt from *Salt Marshes and Protector of Land and Animals* from *The Florida Water Story: From Raindrops to the Sea,* by Peggy Sias Lantz and Wendy A. Hale. Copyright © 1998 by Peggy Sias Lantz and Wendy A. Hale. Reprinted by permission of Pineapple Press, Inc.
Excerpt from *Comets, Meteors, and Asteroids,* by Seymour Simon. Copyright © 1994 by Seymour Simon. Reprinted by permission of William Morrow and Company, an imprint of HarperCollins Publishers.
Earth Changed in Meteor's Fiery Death from *Earth Shake: Poems From the Ground Up,* by Lisa Westberg Peters, Illustrated by Cathie Felstead. Text copyright © 2003 by Lisa Westberg Peters, illustrations copyright 2003 by Cathie Felstead. Reprinted by permission of HarperCollins Publishers.

Photography:

Front and back cover (tiger) © Joe McDonald/Corbis. (front cover bkgd) © Randy Wells/Corbis. **Spine** © PhotoDisc, Inc./Getty Images. **Page iv** © Mark Tomalty/Masterfile Stock Photo Library. **v** © Corbis/Punch Stock. **vi** © William Manning/Corbis. **vii** Courtesy of NASA. **viii** © Dorling Kindersley Picture Library. **ix** © Fukuhara, Inc./Corbis. **ix** © Fukuhara, Inc./Corbis. **S1** © LB Goodman/Omni-Photo Communications. **S2** Courtesy of Dr. Dale Brown Emeagwali. **S2-3** © Microfield Scientific Ltd./Photo Researchers, Inc. **S3** (r) © Alamy Images. **S4-5** (bkgd) © Picimpact/Corbis. Ocelot © Pete Oxford/Nature Picture Library. **S6** (bkgd) © Marc Muench/Muench Photography, Inc. **S9** (bkgd) © HMCo. **S10** (b) © Cassandra Wagner. **S10** (t) © Mitsuhiko Imamori/Minden Pictures. **S11** © Janet Hostetter/AP/Wide World Photos. **S12-13** (b) © Brand X Pictures/Punch Stock. **S12-13** (bkgd) © PhotoDisc, Inc./Punch Stock. **S14** © Stephen Frink/Corbis. **Unit A Opener pages** © Tom Adams/Visuals Unlimited, Inc. **A2-3** © David McCarthy/Science Photo Library/Photo Researchers, Inc. **A3** (1) © Leonard Lessin/Peter Arnold, Inc. **A3** (2) © VVG/Science Photo Library/Photo Researchers, Inc. **A3** (3) © Edward AM Snijde/Lonely Planet. **A3** (4) © Ariel Skelley/Corbis. **A4-5** © Mitsuaki Iwago/Minden Pictures. **A6** (l) © Omikron/Photo Researchers, Inc. **A6** (r) © The Granger Collection, New York. **A7** (b) © Dennis Kunkel Microscopy, Inc. **A7** (t) © Mark Tomalty/Masterfile Stock Photo Library. **A8** © Andrew Syred/Science Photo Library/Photo Researchers, Inc. **A9** © Dr. Gopal Murti/Photo Researchers, Inc. **A10** (b) © CNRI/Science Photo Library/Photo Researchers, Inc. **A10** (c) © Professors P. Motta & T. Naguro/Science Photo Library/Photo Researchers, Inc. **A10** (t) © Dr. Jeremy Burgess/Science Photo Library/Photo Researchers, Inc. **A11** (1) © Omikron/Photo Researchers, Inc. **A11** (2) © Leonard Lessin/Peter Arnold, Inc. **A11** (3) © Dr. Gopal Murti/Photo Researchers, Inc. **A11** (4) © Andrew Syred/Science Photo Library/Photo Researchers, Inc. **A12** © VVG/Science Photo Library/Photo Researchers, Inc. **A12- 13** © Brandon D. Cole/Corbis. **A14** © WG/Science Photo Library/Photo Researchers, Inc. **A15** (b) © Science Photo Library/Photo Researchers, Inc. **A15** (t) © SciMAT/Photo Researchers, Inc. **A16** (b) © Andrew Syred/Science Photo Library/Photo Researchers, Inc. **A16** (t) © Michael Abbey/Visuals Unlimited, Inc. **A17** © Andrew Syred/Science Photo Library/Photo Researchers, Inc. **A18** © Andrew Syred/Photo Researchers, Inc. **A19** (b) © Andrew Syred/Photo Researchers, Inc. **A19** (c) © Andrew Syred/Science Photo Library/Photo Researchers, Inc. **A19** (t) © SciMAT/Photo Researchers, Inc. **A19** © SciMAT/Photo Researchers, Inc. **A20** (b) © The Granger Collection, New York. **A20** (t) © Popperfoto/Alamy Images. **A21** (b) © Index Stock Imagery, Inc. **A21** (t) © Larry Lefever/Grant Heilman Photography. **A22** © Digital Vision/Punch Stock. **A22-23** (bkgd) © Ian Cartwright/PhotoDisc, Inc./Getty Images. **A23** (c) © PhotoDisc, Inc. **A23** (l) © PhotoDisc, Inc. **A23** (r) © PhotoDisc, Inc. **A24** © Duncan Usher/Foto Natura/Minden Pictures. **A25** (1) © SciMAT/Photo Researchers, Inc. **A25** (2) © WG/Science Photo Library/Photo Researchers, Inc. **A25** (3) © RO-MA Stock/Index Stock Imagery. **A25** (4) © Goodshoot/Punch Stock. **A25** (5) © Corbis/Punch Stock. **A26** (b) © Corbis/Punch Stock. **A26** (t) © Kim Taylor and Jane Burton/Dorling Kindersley Picture Library. **A27** (b) © Nick Garbutt/Nature Picture Library. **A27** (t) © Peter Johnson/Corbis. **A28** (b) © Gary Bell/Getty Images. **A28** (t) © Dave Roberts/Science Photo Library/Photo Researchers, Inc. **A30-31** © Dr. David M. Phillips/Visuals Unlimited, Inc. **A32** © Innerspace Imaging/Photo Researchers, Inc. **A35** (b) © Jerry Young/Dorling Kindersley Picture Library. **A35** (t) © Ron Boardman; Frank Lane Picture Agency/Corbis. **A38** © Chris Hellier/Corbis. **A40** © Ariel Skelley/Corbis. **A42-43** © Steve Gschmeissner/Science Photo Library/Photo Researchers, Inc. **A45** (l) © SciMAT/Photo Researchers, Inc. **A45** © Andrew Syred/Science Photo Library/Photo Researchers, Inc. **A46-47** © Steve Hopkin/Getty Images. **A47** (b) Paul McCormick/The Image Bank/Getty Images. **A47** (c) © Eduardo Garcia/Taxi/Getty Images. **A47** (t) © Barry Runk/Stan/Grant Heilman Photography, Inc. **A48-49** © Medford Taylor/National Geographic Society. **A50** © David Sieren/Visuals Unlimited, Inc. **A51** © Barry Runk/Stan/Grant Heilman Photography, Inc. **A52** (l) © Runk/Shoenberger/Grant Heilman Photography, Inc. **A52** (r) © Runk/Shoenberger/Grant Heilman Photography, Inc. **A53** (b) © Andrew Syred/Science Photo Library/Photo Researchers, Inc. **A54** © Claus Meyer/Minden Pictures. **A55** (b) © Claus Meyer/Minden Pictures. **A55** (t) © David Sieren/Visuals Unlimited, Inc. **A57** (l) © PhotoDisc, Inc./Punch Stock. **A57** (r) © Inga Spence/Visuals Unlimited, Inc. **A58** (1) © Alex Kerstitch/Visuals Unlimited, Inc. **A58** (2) © Norbert Wu/Peter Arnold, Inc. **A58** (3) © Ed Reschke/Peter Arnold, Inc. **A58** (4) © Inga Spence/Visuals Unlimited, Inc. **A59** (b) © The Granger Collection, New York. **A59** (t inset) © Patrick Johns/Corbis. **A59** (tr) © Mario Tama/Getty Images. **A60-61** Peter Marbach/Grant Heilman Photography, Inc. **A62** (l) © Richard Cummins/Corbis. **A62** (r) © Dr. Jeremy Burgess/Photo Researchers, Inc. **A63** (b) © Alfred Pasieka/Science Photo Library/Photo Researchers, Inc. **A63** (t) © Sheila Terry/Science Photo Library/Photo Researchers, Inc. **A65** (c) © Alfred Pasieka/Science Photo Library/Photo Researchers, Inc. **A65** (t) © Richard Cummins/Corbis. **A66** © Ed Degginger/Bruce Coleman, Inc. **A66-67** © Digital Vision/Punch Stock. **A68** © Gerald and Buff Corsi/Visuals Unlimited, Inc. **A69** (b) © Brad Mogen/Visuals Unlimited, Inc. **A69** (r) © James Morgan/Dorling Kindersley Picture Library. **A69** (t) © Brad Mogen/Visuals Unlimited, Inc. **A72** (b) © Dwight Kuhn/Bruce Coleman, Inc. **A72** (t) © Peter Steyn/Photo Access/Taxi/Getty Images. **A73** (bl) © Georgette Douwma/The Image Bank/Getty Images. **A73** (br) © Steve Maslowski/Photo Researchers, Inc. **A73** (t) © Lynn Ponto-Peterson. **A74** (bl) © Inga Spence/Visuals Unlimited, Inc. **A74** (br) © Davies & Starr/Stone/Getty Images. **A74** (cl) © Mark Tomalty/Masterfile Stock Photo Library. **A74** (cr) © Rick Souders/Food Pix. **A74** (tl) © Dwight Kuhn. **A74** (tr) © Lois Ellen Frank/Corbis. **A76-77** © Dr. Jeremy Burgess/Science Photo Library/Photo Researchers, Inc. **A76** (c) © Claude Nuridsany & Marie Perennou/Science Photo Library/Photo Researchers, Inc. **A80-81** © Allen Russell/Index Stock Imagery. **A81** (b) © George Grall/National Geographic Image Collection **A81** (t) © Rod Williams/Nature Picture Library. **A82** © Paul Eekhoff/Masterfile Stock Photo Library. **A82-83** © ImageState/Alamy Images Ltd. **A84** © Robert Stock **A85** (b) © Rod Williams/Nature Picture Library. **A85** (t) © Buzz Pictures/Alamy Images. **A86** © Carolina Biological Supply Company/PhotoTake USA. **A89** (inset) © Kaj R. Svenson/Science Photo Library/Photo Researchers, Inc. **A89** © PhotoDisc, Inc. **A90** © Eye of Science/Photo Researchers, Inc. **A91** (b) © Kaj R. Svenson/Science Photo Library/Photo Researchers, Inc. **A91** (t) © Rod Williams/Nature Picture Library. **A92** (b) © Omikron/Photo Researchers, Inc. **A92** (t) © Photo Researchers, Inc. **A93** © Luis Rico **A94** © Yva Momatiuk/John Eastcott/Minden Pictures. **A94-95** © Prenzel, Fritz/Earth Scenes. **A96** © Wally Eberhart/Visuals Unlimited, Inc. **A97** (b) © Dennis Kunkel Microscopy, Inc. **A97** (t) © Andrew J. Martinez/Photo Researchers, Inc. **A99** (l) © Corel/FotoSearch. **A99** (r) © Ulf Wallin/The Image Bank/Getty Images. **A100** (c) © Davies & Starr/The Image Bank/Getty Images. **A100** (l) © Brand X Pictures/Punch Stock. **A100** (r) © Ed Young/Corbis. **A101** (l) © Peter Cade/Stone/Getty Images. **A101** (r) © PhotoDisc, Inc./Punch Stock. **A102** (bl) © Ruth Cole, Animals Animals. **A102** (br) © Peter Blackwell/Nature Picture Library. **A102** (t) © Jeffrey L. Rotman/Peter Arnold, Inc. **A103** (c) © Zigmund Leszczynski/Animals Animals. **A103** (l) © Mark Moffett/Minden Pictures. **A103** (r) © Gerold and Cynthia Merker/Visuals Unlimited, Inc. **A104** (b) © Gerold and Cynthia Merker/Visuals Unlimited, Inc. **A104** (c) © Peter Cade/Stone/Getty Images. **A104** (t) © Wally Eberhart/Visuals Unlimited, Inc. **A105** (t) © Jim Whitmer. **A105** (b) © Patrick Olear/PhotoEdit, Inc. **A106** © Stephen Green-Armytage. **Unit B Opener first page** ©Tom and Pat Leeson. **Unit B Opener spread** ©Gary Kramer. **B2-3** © Kevin Schafer Photography. **B3** (b) © Dwight Kuhn. **B3** (c) © David Mendelsohn/Masterfile Stock Photo Library. **B3** (t) © Dwight Kuhn. **B4** © George McCarthy/Corbis. **B4-5** © Gary Braasch/Corbis. **B6** © Mark Barrett/Index Stock Imagery. **B6-7** (bkgd) © David Muench/Corbis. **B7** (c) © Jeff Lepore/Photo Researchers, Inc. **B7** (l) © Frans Lanting/Minden Pictures. **B7** (r) © Dwight Kuhn Photography. **B8** © Alexis Rosenfeld/Photo Researchers, Inc. **B9** (b) © Alexis Rosenfeld/Photo Researchers, Inc. **B9** (c) © Dwight Kuhn Photography. **B9** (t) © Mark Barrett/Index Stock Imagery. **B10** © W. Perry Conway/Corbis. **B10-11** © National Geogra[illegible] Society. **B13** (b) © Darrell Gulin/Corbis. **B1**[illegible] (deer) © Stephen J. Krasemann/Photo Researchers, Inc. **B13** (t) © Kevin Scha[illegible] Photography. **B13** (toucan) © Cyril L[illegible]

Dorling Kindersley Picture Library. **B14** (b) © Corbis/Punch Stock. **B14** (gila) © Jerry Young/ Dorling Kindersley Photo Library **B14**. (lion) © Kevin Schafer Photography. **B14** (t) © Corbis/ Punch Stock. **B15** (b) © Charles Mauzy/Corbis. **B15** (moose) © Ron Sanford/Corbis. **B15** (t) © Charles Mauzy/Corbis. **B15** (wolf) © Lynn Rogers/Peter Arnold, Inc. **B16** (l) © Stuart Westmorland/Corbis. **B16** (r) © Corbis/Punch Stock. **B17** (br) © Norbert Wu/Minden Pictures. **B17** (l) © Corbis/Punch Stock. **B17** (tr) © Klein/ Peter Arnold, Inc. **B18** (b) © Michio Hoshino/ Minden Pictures. **B18** (inset) © Corbis/Punch Stock. **B19** (b) © Stuart Westmorland/Corbis. **B19** (c) © Ron Sanford/Corbis. **B19** (t) © Corbis/ Punch Stock. **B20-21** (bkgd) © Jeff Greenberg/ Index Stock Imagery, Inc. **B22** (owl) © Joe McDonald/Corbis. **B22** (tree stump) © Corbis. **B22-21** © David Muench/Corbis. **B23** © K Yamashita/PanStock/Panoramic Images/ National Geographic Society. **B24** (inset) © Charles W. Mann/Photo Researchers, Inc. **B24-25** © Kim Taylor and Jane Burton/Dorling Kindersley Picture Library. **B25** (c) © Klein/ Peter Arnold, Inc. **B25** (l) © George McCarthy/ Corbis. **B25** (r) © Michael Gadomski/Animals Animals. **B29** © Kim Taylor and Jane Burton/ Dorling Kindersley Picture Library. **B30-31** © Tom & Pat Leeson Photography. **B31** (t) © Anup Shah/Nature Picture Library. **B34-35** © James L. Amos/Corbis. **B35** (b) © Ron Watts/ Corbis. **B35** (c) © Frank Lane Picture Agency/ Corbis. **B35** (t) © O. Alamany & Vicens/Corbis. **B36-37** © Fred Bavendam/Minden Pictures. **B38** (inset) © Paul A. Souders/Corbis. **B38-39** © K Yamashita/PanStock/Panoramic Images/ National Geographic Society. **B40** (b) © Willis Anderson/Acclaim Images. **B40** (c) © Norbert Wu/Minden Pictures. **B40** (t) © Tom Brakefield/ Corbis. **B41** (b) © Art Twomey/Photo Researchers, Inc. **B41** (t) © Arthur Morris/ Corbis. **B42** (c) © Craig K. Lorenz/Photo Researchers, Inc. **B42** (l) © Dennis Kunkel Microscopy, Inc. **B42** (r) © Chris Newbert/ Minden Pictures. **B43** (b) © Chris Newbert/ Minden Pictures. **B43** (c) © Art Twomey/Photo Researchers, Inc. **B43** (t) © K. Yamashita/ PanStock/Panoramic Images/National Geographic Society. **B44** © Galen Rowell/ Corbis. **B44-45** © Mattias Klum/National Geographic Image Collection. **B46** © Michael & Patricia Fogden/Corbis. **B47** © Michael Quinton/Minden Pictures. **B48** (bl) © James E. Appleby/University of Illinois. **B48** (inset) © Barbara Strnadova/Photo Researchers, Inc. **B48** (t) © Barry Runk/Stan/Grant Heilman Photography. **B49** (inset) © PhotoDisc, Inc./ Punch Stock. **B49** © Layne Kennedy/Corbis. **B50** (b) © Kevin Schafer/Corbis. **B50** (t) © Michael & Patricia Fogden/Corbis. **B51** © Craig Aurness/ Corbis. **B53** (b) © Michael & Patricia Fogden/ Corbis. **B53** (c) © PhotoDisc, Inc./Punch Stock. **B53** (t) © Michael & Patricia Fogden/Corbis. **B54** © Roger Ressmeyer/Corbis. **B56-57** © W. Perry Conway/Corbis. **B58** © Wayne Lawler/ Ecoscene. **B59** (inset) © Alan Pitcairn/Grant Heilman Photography, Inc. **B59** © Alex Maclean/Science Photo Library/Photo Researchers, Inc. **B60** (b) © PhotoDisc, Inc./ Punch Stock. **B60** (c) © Benelux Press/Taxi/Getty Images. **B60** (t) © J.W.Cody/Corbis. **B61** © Jason Hawkes/Corbis. **B62** (b) © Theo Allofs/Corbis. **B62** (c) © David Frazier. **B62** (t) © W. Wayne Lockwood, M.D./Corbis. **B63** (bl) © Ryan/Beyer/ Stone/Getty Images. **B63** (br) © Joseph Sohm/ Corbis. **B63** (inset) © Brandon Cole/Corbis. **B63** (tl) © Gabe Palmer/Corbis. **B63** (tr) © Roger Ressmeyer/Corbis. **B64** (b) © Gabe Palmer/ Corbis. **B64** (c) © Jason Hawkes/Corbis. **B64** (t) © Alan Pitcairn/Grant Heilman Photography, Inc. **B65** (bkgd) © ACE Photo Agency/ Robertstock. **B65** (t) © Dorling Kindersley Picture Library. **B66-67** © National Geographic/ Getty Images. **B68** © John Cancalosi/Peter Arnold, Inc. **Unit C Opener first page** © Rudolf B. Husar/National Geographic Image Collection. **Unit C Opener spread** © Craig Aurness/Corbis. **C2-3** © Corbis. **C3** (b) © Dennis Faulkner/Corbis. **C3** (c) © George F. Mobley/ National Geographic Society Image Collection. **C3** (t) © William Manning/Corbis. **C4-5** © Galen Rowell and Odyssey Productions, Inc. **C6** © Corbis. **C7** (l) © Phil Degginger/Earth Scenes. **C7** (r) © Michael P. Gadomski/Photo Researchers, Inc. **C8** (l) © Kelly-Mooney Photography/Corbis. **C8** (r) © Tony Arruza/ Corbis. **C9** © Captain Albert E. Theberge, Courtesy of NOAA. **C10** © Dr. Ken MacDonald/ Photo Researchers, Inc. **C11** © Captain Albert E. Theberge, Courtesy of NOAA. **C12-13** © Sitki Tarlan/Panoramic Images/National Geographic Society Image Collection. **C14** © Psihoyos/IPN. **C15** © Bob Krist/Corbis. **C16** (b) © Liu Liqun/ Corbis. **C16** (t) © Dale Jorgensen/Superstock, Inc. **C17** (l) © David Muench/Corbis. **C17** (r) © Joe MacDonald/Visuals Unlimited, Inc. **C18** (b) © A. Ramey/PhotoEdit, Inc. **C18** (t) © AP/Wide World Photos. **C19** (1) © Liu Liqun/Corbis. **C19** (2) © Psihoyos/IPN. **C19** (3) © Joe MacDonald/ Visuals Unlimited, Inc. **C19** (4) © AP/Wide World Photos. **C20** © Joan Iaconetti/Bruce Coleman, Inc. **C21** © Gian Berto Vanni/Corbis. **C22-23** © Dave G. Houser/Corbis. **C24** © Geoffrey Clifford/ASA/IPN. **C25** (b) © Andre Bartschi/Wild Tropix. **C25** (t) © Marli Miller, University of Oregon/American Geological Institute. **C26** Courtesy of NASA. **C27** © Jean-Pierre Pieuchot/The Image Bank/Getty Images. **C28** (b) © Ed Darack/Visuals Unlimited, Inc. **C28** (t) © Tom Bean/Corbis. **C29** (b) © Ed Darack/ Visuals Unlimited, Inc. **C29** (c) Courtesy of NASA. **C29** (t) © Marli Miller, University of Oregon/American Geological Institute. **C30-31** © Ron Watts/Corbis.**C34-35** © Gary Braasch/ Corbis. **C35** (b) © William Manning/Corbis. **C35** (c) © Michael S. Yamashita/Corbis. **C35** (t) © Jim Sugar/Corbis. **C36-37** © PhotoDisc, Inc./ Punch Stock. **C38** (l) © Martin B. Withers; Frank Lane Picture Agency/Corbis. **C38** (r) © Bettmann/Corbis. **C39** © Corbis. **C44** (c) © Wolfgang Kaehler/Corbis. **C44** (l) © George D. Lepp/Corbis. **C45** © Wolfgang Kaehler/Corbis. **C50-51** (b) © Peter Carsten/National Geographic Society. **C50-51** (bkgd) © Peter Carsten/ National Geographic Society. **C52** (c) © Reuters/Corbis. **C52** (l) © David Parker/Photo Researchers, Inc. **C54** © Anat Givon/AP/Wide World Photos. **C56** © Jim Sugar/Corbis. **C59** (c) © Jim Sugar/Corbis. **C59** (t) © Anat Givon/AP/ Wide World Photos. **C60-61** © Paul A. Souders/ Corbis. **C62** © Panorama Images/The Image Works. **C63** © Jim Wark/Air Photo. **C64** © Doud Sokell/Visuals Unlimited, Inc. **C66** USGS. **C72-73** © W. Cody/Corbis. **C73** (b) © Richard Hutchings/PhotoEdit, Inc. **C73** (c) © San Bernardino Sun/Corbis Sygma. **C73** (t) © Auto Imagery, Inc. **C74-75** © EyeWire/PhotoDisc, Inc./ Punch Stock. **C76** (b) © Ron Giling/Peter Arnold, Inc. **C76** (c) © Kaj R. Svensson/Science Photo Library/Photo Researchers, Inc. **C78** © Julien Frebet/Peter Arnold, Inc. **C79** (b) © Corbis/Punch Stock. **C79** (c) © AFP Photo/Jeff Haynes/Getty Images. **C79** (t) © Russ Curtis/ Photo Researchers, Inc. **C80** © Joseph Sohm/ Corbis. **C81** (b) © AFP Photo/Jeff Haynes/Getty Images. **C81** (c) © Corbis/Punch Stock. **C81** (t) © Ron Giling/Peter Arnold, Inc. **C82** (l) © John Neubauer/PhotoEdit, Inc. **C82-83** (r) © Reuters/ Corbis. **C84** (l) (m) © Sheila Terry/Science Photo Library. (r) © Corbis. **C84-85** © Sunniva Harte/ Garden Picture Library. **C86** (b) © Lee Foster/ Bruce Coleman, Inc. **C87** © Jim Brandenburg/ Minden Pictures. **C88** © Doug Wechsler/Earth Scenes. **C89** © Larry Lefever/Grant Heilman Photography, Inc. **C90** © Three Lions/Getty Images. **C91** (b) © Three Lions/Getty Images. **C91** (c) © Doug Wechsler/Earth Scenes. **C91** (t) © Jim Brandenburg/Minden Pictures. **C92-93** © MetaCreations/Kai Power Photos. **C94** © Billy Barnes/Transparencies, Inc. **C95** (t) © Anne Dowie/Index Stock Imagery. **C96** (c) © Billy Barnes/Transparencies, Inc. **C97** (t) © Gibson Stock Photography. **C97** (b) © Arthur C. Smith III/Grant Heilman Photography. **C98-99** © Jose Azel/Aurora. **C99** © The Mobile Press Register, Inc. **C103** © Billy Barnes/Transparencies, Inc. **Unit D Opener first page** © Tim Brown/Stone/ Getty Images. **Unit D Opener spread** © CFHT/ Photo Researchers, Inc. **D2-3** © PhotoDisc, Inc./ Punch Stock. **D3** (b) © NASA/Photo Researchers, Inc. **D3** (t) © Schafer & Hill/Peter Arnold, Inc. **D4** (b) © Wallace Garrison/Index Stock Imagery. **D4-5** (bkgd) © Robert Frerck and Odyssey Productions, Inc. **D7** (b) © John Foster/ Masterfile Stock Photo Library. **D7** (c) © Bob Krist/Corbis. **D7** (t) © Chris Cheadle/The Image Bank/Getty Images. **D11** © Chris Cheadle/The Image Bank/Getty Images. **D12** (1) © Adam Jones/Photo Researchers, Inc. . **D12** (2) © David R. Frazier/Photo Researchers, Inc. **D12** (3) © Ray Ellis/Photo Researchers, Inc. **D12** (4) © Digital Vision/Punck Stock. **D12** (t) © National Portrait Gallery, London. **D12-13** (bkgd) © Corbis. **D13** © Dr. June Bacon-Bercey. **D14-15** (bkgd) © David Muench/Corbis. **D17** © Pete Turner/The Image Bank/Getty Images. **D19** (b) © Boyd Norton/The Image Works. **D19** (t) © Jochen Tack/Peter Arnold, Inc. **D21** (b) Courtesy of NOAA. **D21** (c) Courtesy of NOAA. **D21** (t) Courtesy of NOAA. **D22** (1) © Barry Runk/Stan/Grant Heilman Photography. **D22** (2) © Stephen Oliver/Dorling Kindersley Picture Library. **D22** (3) © Karl Shone/Dorling Kindersley Picture Library. **D22** (4) © L.S. Stepanowicz/Bruce Coleman, Inc. **D22** (t) © Denny Eilers/Grant Heilman Photography. **D23** (b) © Karl Shone/Dorling Kindersley Picture Library. **D23** (t) © Pete Turner/The Image Bank/ Getty Images. **D24-25** © Warren Faidley/ Weatherstock. **D27** Courtesy of NOAA. **D28** Courtesy of NASA. **D29** (b) Courtesy of NASA, JPL/Caltech. **D29** (t) © Rob Howard/Corbis. **D30** © Roy Morsch/Corbis. **D30** © Comstock Images. **D38-39** © Bob Krist/Corbis. **D40-41** Courtesy of NASA. **D42** © Darrell Gulin/Corbis. **D43** © MPI/ Getty Images. **D44** Courtesy of NASA/SOHO/ EITD. **D45** (All moon cycle photos) © Larry Landolfi/Photo Researchers, Inc. **D46** (b) © John Chumack/Photo Researchers, Inc. **D46** (t) © Roger Ressmeyer/Corbis. **D47** (b) © Roger Ressmeyer/Corbis. **D47** (c) © Larry Landolfi/ Photo Researchers, Inc. **D47** (t) © Darrell Gulin/ Corbis. **D48-49** Courtesy of NASA. **D51** © Larry Landolfi/Photo Researchers, Inc. **D52-53** Courtesy of NASA, Marshall Space Flight Center. **D53** (b) © Robert Gendler/Science Photo Library. **D53** (c) © Corbis Sygma. **D53** (t) © Jonathan Burnett/Science Photo Library/ Photo Researchers, Inc. **D54-55** Courtesy of NASA, JPL/Caltech. **D58** (Ariel) Courtesy of NASA. **D58** (Enceladus) Courtesy of NASA, JPL/ Caltech. **D58** (lo) © USGS/Photo Researchers, Inc. **D58** (tl) © NASA/Science Source/Photo Researchers, Inc. **D58** (b) © Scott Tysick/ Masterfile Stock Photo Library. **D59** © Jerry Lodriguss/Science Photo Library/Photo Researchers, Inc. **D60** (inset) © Jerry Lodriguss/ Photo Researchers, Inc. **D60** © David Parker/ Photo Researchers, Inc. **D61** (b) © Jerry Lodriguss/Photo Researchers, Inc. **D61** (t) ©

USGS/Photo Researchers, Inc. **D62** Courtesy of NASA. **D62-63** © Fred Espenak/Photo Researchers, Inc. **D64** (bc) © Calvin J. Hamilton. **D64** (bl) © John Chumack/Photo Researchers, Inc. **D64** (br) © Corbis. **D65** (b) Courtesy of NASA, Langley Research Center. **D65** (t) Courtesy of NASA. **D66** (l) Courtesy of NASA. **D66** (r) Courtesy of NASA. **D67** (bl) Courtesy of NASA, JPL/Caltech. **D67** (br) Courtesy of NASA, JPL/Caltech. **D67** (br) © Detlev Vav Ravenswaу/Science Photo Library/Photo Researchers, Inc. **D68** (b)Courtesy of NASA, JPL/Caltech. **D68** (tl) © European Space Agency ESA Handout/Reuters/Corbis. **D69** (b) Courtesy of NASA, JPL/Caltech. **D69** (c) Courtesy of NASA. **D69** (t) © Corbis. **D71** (bkgd) © Dennis Di Cicco/Peter Arnold, Inc. **D72-73** © Canada-France-Hawaii Telescope/Jean Charles Cuillandre/Science Photo Library/Photo Researchers, Inc. **D74** Courtesy of NASA/SOHO/EIT. **D75** © Jerry Schad/Photo Researchers, Inc. **D79** (b) Courtesy of NASA, The Hubble Heritage Team. **D79** (c) Courtesy of NASA, Goddard Space Flight Center. **D79** (t) Courtesy of NASA, Goddard Space Flight Center. **D80** (b) Courtesy of NASA, Goddard Space Flight Center. **D80** (t) © Jerry Schad/Photo Researchers, Inc. **D81** (inset) © Rob Crandall/Stock Connection/IPN. **D81** (bkgd) Courtesy of NASA, Marshall Space Flight Center. **D82-83** Courtesy of NASA. **D85** Courtesy of NASA, The Hubble Heritage Team. **Unit E Opener first page** © Rob Casey/Stone/Getty Images. **Unit E Opener spread** © John William Banagan/The Image Bank/Getty Images. **E2-3** © Bob Gomel/Corbis. **E3** (b) © Corel. **E3** (c) © Archivo Iconografico, S.A./Corbis. **E3** (t) © Mark Garlick/Science Photo Library/Photo Researchers, Inc. **E4-5** © Lester Lefkow/Corbis. **E6** © The Granger Collection, New York. **E8** (l) © Barry Runk/Stan/Grant Heilman Photography, Inc. **E9** © Lawrence Lawry/Science Photo Library/Photo Researchers, Inc. **E10** (1) © PhotoDisc, Inc. **E10** (2) © Eyewire/Photodisc, Inc./Punch Stock. **E10** (3) © Photolibrary. Ltd./Index Stock Imagery. **E10** (4) © Comstock Images/Alamy Images. **E11** © Comstock Images/Alamy Images Ltd. **E12-13** © Terry Macnamara. **E15** (l) © The Granger Collection, New York. **E15** (r) © Science Museum/Science and Society Picture Library. **E18** (bananas) © Comstock. **E18** (fireworks) © G. Brad Lewis/Science Photo Library/Photo Researchers, Inc. **E18** (magnesium) © Earth Scenes. **E18** (potassium) © Andrew Lambert Photography/Science Photo Library/Photo Researchers, Inc. **E19** (calcium) © Charles D. Winters/Photo Researchers, Inc. **E19** (chip) © Joel Greenstein/Omni-Photo Communications. **E19** (silicon) © R-R/Grant Heilman Photography, Inc. **E20** (b) © Norman Tomalin/Bruce Coleman, Inc. **E20** (inset) © Andrew Lambert Photography/Science Photo Library/Photo Researchers, Inc. **E20** (t) © Burr Lewis/Democrat and Chronicle/AP Wide World Photo. **E21** © Science Museum/Science and Society Picture Library. **E22** (b) © Science Photo Library/Photo Researchers, Inc. **E22** (t) © Dr. H. Juanita Harper. **E23** (b) © Dr. Katharina Lodders. **E23** (t) © Dr. Mario J. Molina. **E24-25** © Dave Bartruff/Index Stock Imagery. **E26** © Jack Anderson/Picture Arts/Corbis. **E27** (b) © Ton Koene/Visuals Unlimited, Inc. **E27** (t) © Adam Wolfitt/Corbis. **E30** © Richard Megna/Fundamental Photographs. **E31** (b) © Dave King/Dorling Kindersley Picture Library. **E31** (c) © Peter Harholdt/Corbis. **E31** (t) © David Wrobel/Visuals Unlimited, Inc. **E32** © Raymond Tercafs-Production Services/Bruce Coleman, Inc. **E33** © Richard Megna/Fundamental Photographs. **E34** © Philadelphia Museum of Art/Corbis. **E35** © Ira Block/National Geographic Society. **E38-39** © Zoran Milich/Masterfile Stock Photography. **E39** (b) © PhotoDisc, Inc. **E39** (c) © Peter Skinner/Photo Researchers, Inc. **E39** (t) © Jim Cummins/Taxi/Getty Images. **E40** © Stephen Oliver/Dorling Kindersley Picture Library. **E40-41** © Mark Tomalty/Masterfile Stock Photo Library. **E46** © Sheila Terry/Science Photo Library/Photo Researchers, Inc. **E49** © Linda Pitkin/Taxi/Getty Images. **E53** (b) © Larry Stepanowicz/Visuals Unlimited, Inc. **E53** © MedioImages/Punch Stock. **E54** © Somboon-UNEP/Peter Arnold, Inc. **E56** (All) © Wally Eberhart/Visuals Unlimited, Inc. Inc. **E57** (b) © Wally Eberhart/Visuals Unlimited, Inc. **E57** (c) © Larry Stepanowicz/Visuals Unlimited, Inc. **E58-59** © PhotoDisc, Inc. **E60** © Food Collection/Punch Stock. **E62** © Lawrence Stepanowicz/Panographics. **E62** © Lawrence Stepanowicz/Panographics. **E63** (bl) © Angelo Cavalli/Index Stock Imagery. **E63** (br) © Mauro Fermariello/Science Photo Library/Photo Researchers, Inc. **E63** (cr) © Philip Gould/Corbis. **E63** (tr) © Jeremy Bishop/Science Photo Library/Photo Researchers, Inc. **E64** (c) © Firefly Productions/Corbis. **E64** (l) © Tony Freeman/PhotoEdit, Inc. **E65** (b) © Tony Freeman/PhotoEdit, Inc. **E65** (c) © Lawrence Stepanowicz/Panographics. **E65** (t) © Food Collection/Punch Stock. **E66-67** © Richard D. Fisher. **E67** © Maurice Nimmo; Frank Lane Picture Agency/Corbis. **E70-71** © Annie Griffiths Belt/Corbis. **E71** (b) © Dorling Kindersley Picture Library. **E71** (t) © Ralph A. Clevenger/Corbis. **E72** © Jeff Sherman/Getty Images. **E72-73** © Alvis Upitis/Getty Images. **E74-75** © Russell Monk/Masterfile Stock Photo Library. **E76** © Allsport Concepts/Getty Images. **E77** © Fundamental Photographs. **E78** (All) © Fundamental Photographs. **E79** © Russell Monk/Masterfile Stock Photo Library. **E81** (bc) © Tim Wright/Corbis. **E81** (bkgd) © James L. Amos/Peter Arnold, Inc. **E81** (tl) © Jens Buettner/dpa/Landov. **E84** © Roy Toft/National Geographic Image Collection. **E85** © Michael Alberstat/Masterfile Stock Photo Library. **E86** (t) © Bill Boch/Botanica/Getty Images. **E87** (b) © Tom Uhlman/Visuals Unlimited, Inc. **E87** (t) © HMCo./Fundamental Photographs. **E88** (1) © Roy Toft/National Geographic Image Collection. **E88** (2) © Michael Alberstat/Masterfile Stock Photo Library. **E88** (3) © Fundamental Photographs. **E88** (4) © Tom Uhlman/Visuals Unlimited, Inc. **E89** (bkgd) © PhotoDisc, Inc. **E89** (bkgd) © MetaCreations/Kai Power Photos. **E89** (bkgd) © MetaCreations/Kai Power Photos. **E89** (t) © Dwayne Newton/PhotoEdit, Inc. **E90-91** © Richard Menga/Fundamental Photographs, NYC. **Unit F Opener first page** © ER Degginger/Color-Pic, Inc. **Unit F Opener spread** ©Warren Faidley/Weatherstock. **F2-3** (bkgd) © Auto Imagery, Inc. **F3** (b) © Alex Bartel/Photo Researchers, Inc. **F3** (c) © Peter Adams/Index Stock Imagery. **F3** (t) © Reuters/Corbis. **F4-5** © ImageState-Pictor/PictureQuest. **F7** © Brand-X Pictures/Punch Stock. **F8** © Heinz Kluetmeier/Sports Illustrated/Figure Skater Brian Boitano, 1988. **F9** (1) © Osf/M. Hill/Animals Animals. **F9** (2) © Phillip Colla/SeaPics. **F9** (3) © Mark Payne-Gill/Nature Picture Library. **F9** (4) © Nancy Rotenberg/Animals Animals. **F12** (bc) © Michael Newman/PhotoEdit, Inc. **F12** (bl) © Michael Newman/PhotoEdit, Inc. **F13** (b) © Michael Newman/PhotoEdit, Inc. **F13** (t) © Brand-X Pictures/Punch Stock. **F14-15** © Images on the Wild Side/Denver Bryan. **F17** © Digital Vision/Punch Stock. **F19** (b) © Dorling Kindersley Picture Library. **F19** (c) © Dorling Kindersley Picture Library. **F19** (t) © Dorling Kindersley Picture Library. **F21** © Michael Newman/PhotoEdit, Inc. **F22** (bc) © Jeffrey Greenberg/Photo Researchers, Inc. **F22** (bl) © Jeffrey Greenberg/Photo Researchers, Inc. **F23** (t) © Ned Therrien/Visuals Unlimited, Inc. **F24** (1) © Artville. **F24** (2) © Phil Crabbe/Dorling Kindersley Picture Library. **F24** (3) © Novastock/PhotoEdit, Inc. **F24** (4) © Brand X Pictures/Alamy Images. **F25** (b) © Artville. **F25** (c) © Michael Newman/PhotoEdit, Inc. **F26** (b) © Dorling Kindersley Picture Library. **F26** (t) © The Granger Collection, New York. **F27** (bl) © The Granger Collection, New York. **F27** (l) © The Granger Collection, New York. **F27** (r) Courtesy of NASA, Johnson Space Center. **F27** (tr) Courtesy of NASA, Johnson Space Center. **F27** © Popperfoto. **F27** © CPL/Popperfoto/Retrofile. **F31** © Spencer Grant/PhotoEdit, Inc. **F31** © Spencer Grant/PhotoEdit, Inc. **F33** © Van Dykes Restorers. **F34** (l) © Chris Madeley/Science Photo Library/Photo Researchers, Inc. **F35** (b) © Van Dykes Restorers. **F36-37** © AP Photo/Str. **F39** © Brand-X Pictures/Punch Stock. **F40-41** (bkgd) © Stone/Getty. **F41** (b) © Imtek Imagineering/Masterfile. **F41** (c) © David Young-Wolff/PhotoEdit, Inc. **F41** (t) © Doug Martin/Photo Researchers, Inc. **F42-43** © Fukuhara, Inc/Corbis. **F44** © Bob Daemmerich/Corbis. **F45** © Corbis. **F47** © Courtesy of Mercury Marine Company. **F48** © Loren M. Winters. **F49** (b) © Loren M. Winters. **F49** (t) © Corbis. **F50** © Joseph Van Os/The Image Bank/Getty Images. **F50-51** (bkgd) © Carl & Ann Purcell/Corbis. **F54** © Phil McCarter/PhotoEdit, Inc. **F55** © Corbis. **F56** © ACE Photo Agency/Robertstock. **F57** (engine) © Ben Li/Corbis. **F57** (man) © Corbis. **F58** (l) © View Pictures Ltd./Alamy Images. **F58** (r) © Gibson Stock Photography. **F59** (b) © View Pictures Ltd./Alamy Images. **F59** (c) © Phil McCarter/PhotoEdit, Inc. **F60** Courtesy of United States Navy. **F60** Courtesy of United States Air Force. **F61** © George Hall/Corbis. **F62** (bl) © Stone/Getty Images. **F62-63** (bkgd) © Lucidio Studio Inc./Corbis. **F64** © ACE Photo Agency/Robertstock. **F66** (b) © Churchill and Klehr. **F66** (t) © SIU/Visuals Unlimited, Inc. **F68** (b) © Adam Jones/Visuals Unlimited. **F68** (t) © Stockbyte/SuperStock. **F69** (b) © SIU/Visuals Unlimited, Inc. **F70-71** © NIH/Custom Medical Stock Photo/Science Photo Library/Photo Researchers, Inc. **F70** (b) © Maximilian Stock LTD/Science Photo Library/Photo Researchers, Inc. **F73** © ACE Photo Agency/Robertstock. **F74-75** Courtesy of the U.S. Navy. **F75** (b) © Ted Kinsman/PhotoReseachers, Inc. **F75** (t) © Robert Llewellyn/PictureQuest. **F76-77** (bkgd) © David Young Wolff/PhotoEdit, Inc. **F79** (1) © David Young Wolff/PhotoEdit, Inc. **F79** (2) © Comstock Images/Getty. **F79** (3) © Japack Company/Corbis. **F82** © Creatas. **F83** (b) © Creatas/PunchStock. **F84** © Bettmann/Corbis. **F86** © P. Sancho/Masterfile Stock Photo Library. **F86-87** (bkgd) © Udo Frank/Photosights. **F89** (br) © Rick Berkowitz/Index Stock Photography. **F90** (l) © Kindra Clineff/PictureQuest. **F90** (r) © Joerg Mueller/Visum/The Image Works. **F92** (bl) © Richard T. Nowitz/Corbis. **F92** (br) © Cyril Laubscher/Dorling Kindersley Picture Library. **F93** (l) © Ted Kinsman/Photo Researchers, Inc. **F93** (r) © Tony Freeman/PhotoEdit, Inc. **F95** (b) © Cyril Laubscher/Dorling Kindersley Picture Library. **F96-97** Courtesy of NASA. **F99** © PhotoDisc, Inc./Punch Stock. **F100-101** © Scott Kerrigan. **F101** (b) © Brian Hagiwara/FoodPix/Getty Images. **F101** (c) © Corbis. **F101** (t) © Wolfgang Kaehler/Corbis. **F102** © Michael Melford/The Image Bank/Getty Images. **F102-103** (bkgd) © David R. Frazier/Photo Researchers, Inc. **F106** © Dmitriy

Margolin/D Photography. **F107** (br) © Mike Mullen. **F107** (tr) © Science Photos/Alamy Images Ltd. **F110** © Earl Harper/EcoStock. **F110-111** (bkgd) © Spencer Grant/PhotoEdit, Inc. **F112** © Barrie Rokeach. **F116** (t) © Dennis Boothroyd/EcoStock. **F117** (b) © Will Powers. **F117** (t) © Barrie. **F120** © Bettmann/Corbis. **F121** © Stock Montage/Hulton Archive/Getty Images. **F122-123** (bkgd) © Henrik Sorensen/ The Image Bank/Getty Images. **F124** (l) © Alfred Harrell/Smithsonian Institution. **F124** (r) © Mark Richard/PhotoEdit, Inc. **F125** (b) © Chris Cheadle/The Image Bank/Getty Images. **F125** (t) © Ken Chernus/Taxi/Getty Images. **F126** © Bob Daemmrich/The Image Works. **F128** (t) © Ken Chernus/Taxi/Getty Images. **F129** (bkgd) © Comstock. **F129** (t) © Ted Soqui/ Corbis. **F129** (b) © Michael Newman/PhotoEdit, Inc. **F130-131** © Paul Katz/Index Stock Imagery/ PictureQuest. **H1, H4, H7, H8, H9, H14, H16, H17** © HMCo. **H18** (b) © Goodshoot/Alamy Images. **H19** © PhotoDisc, Inc./Punch Stock. **H22** © Lawrence Maureen/Alamy Images. **H24** (b) © Comstock/Punch Stock. **H25** (t) © Stephen Ogilvy/Alamy Images. **H25** (b) © Michael Newman/PhotoEdit, Inc.

Assignment Photography

© HMCo./Chris Deford: **E57** (t). © HMCo./Sharon Hoogstraten: **C94, C95** (b), **C41**. ©HMCo./ Allan Landau : **S5, S7, S9, S12, S15, A5, A13, A15, A23, A31, A33, A34, A35, A36, A37, A49, A49, A53, A56, A61, A67, A79, A81, A83, A85, A86, A95, A96, B5, B5, B23, B37, B45, B57, C5** (tr), **C5** (tc), **C13** (tr), **C13** (tc), **C13**(br), **C23, C23**(cr), **C37, C51, C61, C75, C85, C92, C93, D5, D5, D14** (b), **D15, D31, D32, D37, D41, D55, D63, D73, E5, E8** (r), **E13, E25** (tr), **E25** (br), **E41** (tr), **E41** (br), **E42, E43, E47** (t), **E48, E51, E52-53, E55, E58, E59, E61, E65, E73, E76** (inset), **E83, F5, F15, F29, F32, F43, F46** (bl), **F49** (c), **F51, F52, F53, F63, F77, F78, F79, F81, F87, F89, F91** (c), **F103, F104, F105, F109, F111, F122, F123, F125** (c). ©HMCo./Lawrence Migdale: **F10, F11, F13** (c), **F16, F23** (b), **F25** (t), **F30.** © HMCo./Charles Winters: **E28** (l), **E28** (r), **E19, E29, E33, E44, E45, E46, E47** (c), **E47** (b), **E54, F80, F88, F92** (t), **F95** (t), **F113, F114, F115, F117** (c). © Manoj Shah/Stone/Getty Images **D33** © HMCo./Coppola Studios Inc.

Illustrations

A9 Bill Melvin. **A16** Bill Melvin. **A18** Steve McEntee. **A32** Bill Melvin. **A33** Bart Vallecoccia. **A34** Joel Ito. **A35** Bart Vallecoccia. **A36** Joel Ito. **A37** (t) Bill Melvin (b) Joel Ito. **A38** Joel Ito. **A39** Bart Vallecoccia. **A40** (t) Joe LeMonnier (b) Joel Dubin. **A41** Joel Ito. **A51** Steve McEntee. **A53** Virge Kask. **A55** Virge Kask. **A56** Bill Melvin. **A64** Virge Kask. **A65** Steve McEntee. **A70** Virge Kask. **A79** Virge Kask. **A87** Laurie O'Keefe. **A88** Laurie O'Keefe. **A89** Laurie O'Keefe. **A91** Laurie O'Keefe. **A94-95** Laurie O'Keefe. **A98-99** Laurie O'Keefe. **A100** Laurie O'Keefe. **A109** Laurie O'Keefe. **A112** Bill Melvin. **A144** Bill Melvin. **B11** Joe LeMonnier. **B12** Joe LeMonnier. **B16-17** Rolin Graphics. **B27** Rolin Graphics. **B28** Rolin Graphics. **B29** Rolin Graphics. **B29** Rolin Graphics. **B51** Bill Melvin. **B52** Joe LeMonnier. **B54-55** Bill Melvin. **B55** Bill Melvin. **B62-63** Joe LeMonnier. **B72** Bill Melvin. **C6** Bill Melvin. **C7** Bill Melvin. **C8** Bill Melvin. **C9** Bill Melvin. **C10** (t) Joe Lemonnier (b) Bill Melvin. **C11** Bill Melvin. **C15** Bill Melvin. **C16** Bill Melvin. **C20** Joe LeMonnier. **C26** Bill Melvin. **C27** Bill Melvin. **C40** Joel Dubin. **C43** Joe LeMonnier. **C45** (t) Joe LeMonnier (b) Joel Dubin. **C46** Drew-Brook-Cormack Assoc. **C53** Joel Dubin. **C54** Joel Dubin. **C55** Joe LeMonnier. **C57** Joel Dubin. **C58** Joe LeMonnier. **C62** Joel Dubin. **C63** Joel Dubin. **C64** Joel Dubin. **C67** (t) Joel Dubin (b) Joe LeMonnier. **C77** Pat Rossi. **C79** Pat Rossi. **C81** Pat Rossi. **C83-84** Bill Melvin. **C87** Pat Rossi. **C88** Pat Rossi. **C97** Joe LeMonnier. **C98** Joe LeMonnier. **C104** Joe LeMonnier. **D6** Slim Films. **D8** Slim Films. **D8-9** Slim Films. **D10** Joe LeMonnier. **D11** Slim Films. **D17** Slim Film. **D18** Joe LeMonnier. **D19** Slim Films. **D20** Joe LeMonnier. **D23** Slim Films. **D34** Slim Films. **D35** Slim Films. **D36** Slim Films. **D37** Slim Films. **D38** Slim Films. **D43** Slim Films. **D45** Slim Films. **D46** Slim Films. **D56** Slim Films. **D59** Slim Films. **D61** Slim Films. **D76-77** Slim Films. **D78** Slim Films. **D80** Slim Films. **D88** Bill Melvin. **E7** Bill Melvin. **E8** Bill Melvin. **E9** Bill Melvin. **E11** Bill Melvin. **E26** Bill Melvin. **E27** Bill Melvin. **E30** Bill Melvin. **E31** Bill Melvin. **E32** Bill Melvin. **E33** George V. Kelvin. **E45** George V. Kelvin. **E48-49** Bill Melvin. **E56** Bill Melvin. **E62** Bill Melvin. **E74** George V. Kelvin. **E75** George V. Kelvin. **E79** George V. Kelvin. **E87** George V. Kelvin. **E96** Bill Melvin. **F6** Bill Melvin. **F17** Bill Melvin. **F18** Bill Melvin. **F20** Bill Melvin. **F21** Bill Melvin. **F22** Bill Melvin. **F23** Bill Melvin. **F30** Ron Carboni. **F33** Bill Melvin. **F34** Slim Films. **F35** Bill Melvin. **F60** Bill Melvin. **F61** Bill Melvin. **F65** Mike Saunders. **F67** Mike Saunders. **F69** Mike Saunders. **F78** George V. Kelvin. **F79** George V. Kelvin. **F83** George V. Kelvin. **F85** Bill Melvin. **F91** George V. Kelvin. **F94** George V. Kelvin. **F95** George V. Kelvin. **F106** Slim Films. **F108** Slim Films. **F109** Slim Films. **F118-119** Drew-Brook-Cormack Association. **F126** Slim Films. **F127** Slim Films. **F128** Slim Films. **F136** Bill Melvin. **H20** Joel Ito. **H21** Bart Vallecoccia.